PRESTON NORTH END THE SEVENTIES

Edward Skingsley

ISBN:
ISBN-13:9781729373392

DEDICATION

To my grandson, Oliver.

CONTENTS

CONTENTS

(continued)

ACKNOWLEDGMENTS

Special thanks to
Mike Hill, Lancashire Post
Ben Rhodes, PNE FC
Kevin Williamson
John Steinson
Ian Rigby
and
Dr David Hunt, author of the reference book *'The History of Preston North End – The Power, the Politics and the People'*

CHAPTER 1

NO EASY TASK

For the North End fan, the Seventies gave us a bit of everything. The go-stop-go-stop start to the decade under Alan Ball Snr was followed abruptly by a complete reverse manoeuvre under Bobby Charlton. The middle years were a period of re-grouping and gentle forward momentum under Harry Catterick, before Nobby Stiles and Alan Kelly drove the club onward and upwards once again as the Eighties loomed. Each of the managers had to work with a resolute board that operated a fixed agenda of its own...and would bow to nobody.

The club was on a high as it kicked off the 1971/72 season safely back in Division Two. Ball had done a fine job in gaining promotion from Division Three at the first attempt and was looking for increased backing from the board for the next part of the journey. Of all the managers at Deepdale during the Seventies, Ball Snr was the one that lived and breathed North End. It really was a love affair.

Remarkably standing in fourth place on December 4th 1971 and in fifth position on the same weekend exactly a year later, each promising campaign would disintegrate into a full scale relegation battle after the new year celebrations - the second time in 1972/73 costing Ball his job. The fans were heavily split on this issue, and there were many protests.

Granted, the form North End had shown since the start of 1973 had been awful. They were suddenly being beaten by huge margins and were in freefall. At a second vote-of-confidence board meeting, all nine directors voted alike to seal Ball's fate. However to sack a man on February 12th 1973 who had been the bookmakers second favourite on December 20th to take over the Manchester United managerial vacancy, did seem very harsh and no doubt broke Ball's heart.

New manager Alan Ball Snr at the North End pre-season photocall, July 1970

Ball certainly had the know-how to take North End forward, and perhaps with a little more patience and help from the board he would have succeeded. He was however becoming increasingly affected by the pressure of the situation at Deepdale...and his chain smoking habit wasn't helping matters.

He had suffered a mild heart attack during the previous 1971/72 season with North End under a relegation cloud. Although this took place during a charity football game, the stress of his job was beginning to tell.

He was becoming more and more outspoken both with opposition fans and the hierarchy within his own club. As he neared the end of his tenure, there were three very public incidents outstanding on his charge sheet, the last being the trading of blows with a Grimsby Town fan after the FA Cup tie at Blundell Park. It's hard to imagine that all this didn't have a bearing on the board's ultimate decision.

Assistant manager Frank Lord stood in for Ball for the remainder of the season.

Bobby Charlton's turn at the pre-season photocall, July 1973

North End survived both of those flirtations with relegation, and when the legendary Bobby Charlton took over for the 1973/74 season, there was mass optimism all around Deepdale and far beyond, as for once the national press latched onto the Lilywhites. North End began slowly, then improved and reached the dizzy heights of second place after nine games before gently falling away over the rest of the season to finish

21st, saying 'hello' to Division Three once again.

Charlton saw two seasons out, then resigned early in the third over *'The John Bird Saga'* - never coming to terms with the logic of the board in agreeing to sell the aforementioned Bird in exchange for Alex Bruce and a wedge of much needed cash. It has to be said that Charlton had brought some decent talent to the club in Francis Burns, David Sadler and of course Nobby Stiles – to name just three. Stiles eventually resigned over the matter too – but was later wooed back by the new manager.

He was Harry Catterick, who had led Everton to League Championship in 1970. He came in just a week after Charlton's departure and started to change the team slowly but surely, no doubt acting on the advice of his coaches. He was well supported by both Stiles (after his return to the club) and reserve team coach Alan Kelly, who were both prominent in developing and bringing in younger players through from the reserve and 'A' team squads when they felt they were ready. Along with a few signings here and there, Catterick certainly steadied the ship during his two seasons in charge.

Harry Catterick (right) and Bill Shankly recalling many a past Merseyside derby in 1975

This took us to the close season of 1976/77, when the board decided that the time was right to give coach Nobby Stiles a chance to hold the first team reigns, ably assisted by Alan Kelly.

This worked out well; Stiles and Kelly took North End to promotion at the first attempt, albeit scraping through in third place. Nevertheless, the club was back in Division Two and built on their new status by registering finishes of seventh in 1978/79 and 10th in 1979/80.

It was a good, solid ending to the Seventies - after all North End were

The North End bench in April 1978. Substitute Steve Doyle, assistant manager Alan Kelly and manager Nobby Stiles

now officially ranked the 32nd best club in the country despite the torrid ups and downs and ravages of the decade.

Thankfully - for their sanity at least - North End's long-suffering and patient fans could not have possibly foreseen what was waiting for them around the corner right from the starting whistle in the early Eighties!

CHAPTER 2

1970/71

A BALL COMES BOUNCING IN

Alan Ball Snr arrived at Deepdale with North End at their lowest point in their proud history. Appointed after impressing the board with his frankness, willingness to 'get stuck in' and to solve the clubs' on-field problems, his work could not have been bettered by any other manager in the land.

North End returned to Division Two as champions after his first season in charge; his team played an exciting brand of football utilising a strong defence, artistic midfield, pacey wingers and productive strikers.

During the sluggish start to that 1970/71 campaign, nobody in their wildest dreams could have imagined how dramatically the very end of the season would unfold, with an away win at table toppers Fulham to seal promotion, quickly followed by a home win against Rotherham United to go one further and lift the championship trophy.

It would be remiss of me to delve too deeply into the performances of Preston North End in that campaign as my first book, *A Season To*

Savour covered that particular season in great depth. I fully understand that we are now in an era of recycling, but that would be taking it all a little bit too far!

However, I have included a review of *Match of the Day*, transmitted on May 1st 1971 that I wrote for BackPass magazine in 2013. The BBC programme covered the epic clash at Craven Cottage between Fulham and North End and was undoubtedly one of the best days in the clubs long history.

This book then continues with some of the best matches of the Alan Ball years from 1971/72, and then progresses through the ups and downs of the decade.

Alan Ball Snr –started the decade by steering North End to promotion in 1970/71

TV Archive
Programme: Match of the Day
Duration: 60 minutes
First Transmitted: BBC1, 10:10pm, 1.5.71
Commentator: Barry Davies

The May 1st 1971 edition of MotD showcased two games; Liverpool v Southampton, the 'starter' and Fulham v Preston North End, the 'main', in what was effectively 'The Third Division title shootout.' Introduced by the brilliant David Coleman, the programme ran the Goal of the Season candidates too – and what a superb selection they were – and the usual news round-up.

The result implications for the game at Craven Cottage were seemingly endless. Fulham, already promoted, needed a just a draw to give them the Championship. For Preston, a win would secure promotion, but a further win at home to Rotherham in their final match, would give them top spot. A draw or defeat for Preston left them exposed to Halifax Town coming up on the rails.

Barry Davies (BD) set the scene for us at Craven Cottage that day. "Newly promoted Fulham are on the way back. They are unchanged after a 3-2 away win at Bradford and Barry Lloyd and Les Barrett remain ever presents. Preston are missing leading scorer Gerry Ingram, Norman Lloyd takes over the number nine shirt."

Preston's Lloyd gets the game underway. Fulham, wishing to please the vocal home support do all of the early attacking, with neat, swift passing movements. A seemingly dangerous attack is ruled out for offside with the Preston goal exposed, but a Graham Hawkins header from a Clive Clark corner registers a 'near miss' at the Fulham end, and seems to encourage North End out of their shell. A well engineered move down the Fulham left between Alex Spark and George Ross sees a great ball played in for the diminutive Bobby Ham who just can't quite wrap his foot around it, and it bobbles into the Fulham keeper's arms.

BD picks up on the changing flow of the game too. "Preston are really beginning to settle down," he tells us prophetically. Spark, Ross and Ricky Heppolette then combine neatly as Preston attack the Fulham left once again. The move is ended by a foul on Spark, and North End's midfield maestro Alan Spavin takes the free kick. A lovely floating ball is aimed to the assembled throng of North Enders in the box, but Stan Horne manages to get the ball out of the way at the expense of a corner.

Preston under Alan Ball Snr, were noted for their imagination at dead ball situations and today was to be no exception. In a move manufactured in heaven, the Clark corner is directed towards the middle of the box, where Norman Lloyd out jumps his marker and flicks the ball backwards using its pace. The increased elevation of the ball takes out the entire line of Fulham defenders leaving Heppolette, lurking behind them to run in to arrow a diving header into the bottom left hand corner of the onion bag. "Oh what a good goal!" shouts BD approvingly, as Hepplolette picks himself up off the floor and receives hugs and kisses from his team mates.

"Preston are proving a point after Fulham's bright start, and are getting better all the time," confirms BD as a Preston move down the Fulham right forces yet another corner. Clark once more swings the ball in and Lloyd sends a looping header goalbound, only to see Fred Callaghan clear off the line.

It's been a frustrating first half for the home side, and this is encapsulated in an extraordinary swing and connect on Spark's shin by Steve Earle, after a push and shove incident near the Preston box. This makes BD's blood boil. "Whatever was done to Earle you cannot condone players kicking each other like that! A thoroughly stupid action by him."

Fulham are ending the first half as they began it. Hawkins, that most solid of defenders, clears away the free kick, but the ball returns with interest, at head height across the line of the six yard box resulting in,

"...a great save by Alan Kelly, he really pulled that out of the air and it stuck to his fingertips." There is time for a great shot by George Johnston to be saved low down by Kelly before half time finally arrives.

Fulham really turn the screw in the second half. They attack both flanks with swift moves, and it's a ball played in by Barrett on the left that sees Kelly risk life and limb at the feet of the oncoming Johnston. When Johnston is then replaced by Vic Halom, the heat is turned up even higher. The increasingly menancing Barrett, now playing in an apparent free role, tees up Halom 15 yards out, but he shoots wide. Barrett then fires in a great cross for Halom to head just over the bar. There is no respite for Preston as their box is bombarded from all directions.

With just under 15 minutes left, Barrett himself is bearing down on goal and fires in a shot that beats Kelly, only to be cleared off the line by Heppolette. Preston are creaking, and the tension for their fans is unbearable.

A midfield punt from Horne finds Barrett on the left, unmarked as the Preston defence is caught rushing out, leaving Kelly alone at the back. Barrett drives to the byline and delivers a superb hard low cross to Kelly's left for Halom to run on to and surely convert. However he is thwarted by an unbelievable lunging tackle by the classy John Bird that is worthy of saving any game.

After a minute or so of injury time, Mr Gow blows the final whistle and the celebrations begin for the Preston team, management and fans. "Preston have their victory and today we have seen the best two teams in the division," BD concludes in his summary. Preston would go onto beat Rotherham United in their final game and be crowned champions a few days later.

For Preston, with such a famous past, but starved of 1960's success, (although remarkably they still stand fourth of 140 clubs in the all-time English League table), it was a season to savour. Local North End fan and writer Jon Roper recalls, *"I have watched PNE since 1967, seen play offs, promotions and championships, but that day and that game in West London is the one I will take with me to my grave."*

Perhaps the final words though should go to the North End skipper Graham Hawkins. After watching the game again, he sent me a text. It simply read *"fantastic memories."*

EDWARD SKINGSLEY relives a tense finish to the Third Division title race in the 1970-71 season ... between Fulham and Preston North End

THE May 1, 1971 edition of *Match of the Day* showcased two games, with Liverpool v Southampton the starter and Fulham v Preston North End the main in what was effectively a Third Division title shoot-out. Introduced by the brilliant David Coleman, the programme ran the Goal of the Season candidates too – and what a superb selection they were – as well as the usual news round-up.

The implications of the game at Craven Cottage were seemingly endless. Fulham, already promoted, needed a just a draw to give them the title. For Preston, a win would secure promotion, and a further win at home to Rotherham in their final match would give them top spot. A draw or defeat for Preston would leave them exposed to Halifax Town coming up on the rails.

Barry Davies sets the scene at Craven Cottage. "Newly promoted Fulham are on the way back. They are unchanged after a 3-2 away win at Bradford and Barry Lloyd and Les Barrett remain ever presents. Preston are missing leading scorer Gerry Ingram. Norman Lloyd takes over the No 9 shirt."

Preston's Lloyd gets the game underway. Fulham do all of the early attacking, with neat, swift passing movements. A seemingly dangerous attack is ruled out for offside with the Preston goal exposed, but a Graham Hawkins header from a Clive Clark corner registers a near miss at the Fulham end, and seems to encourage North End out of their shell.

A well engineered move down the Fulham left between Alex Spark and George Ross sees a great ball played in for the diminutive Bobby Ham, who just can't quite wrap his foot around it, and it bobbles into the Fulham keeper's arms.

Davies picks up on the changing flow of the game too. "Preston are really beginning to settle down," he tells us prophetically. Spark, Ross and Ricky Heppolette then combine neatly as Preston attack the Fulham left once again. The move is ended by a foul on Spark, and North End's midfield maestro Alan Spavin takes the free kick. A lovely floating ball is aimed to the assembled throng of North Enders in the box, but Stan Horne manages to get the ball out of the way at the expense of a corner.

Preston, under Alan Ball senior, were noted for their imagination at dead-ball situations and this game was to be no exception. In a move manufactured in heaven, the Clark corner is directed towards the middle of the box, where Norman Lloyd out jumps his marker and flicks the ball backwards using its pace. The increased elevation of the ball takes out the entire line of Fulham defenders leaving Heppolette, lurking behind them, to run in to arrow a diving header into the bottom left hand corner of the onion bag. "Oh what a good goal!" shouts Davies approvingly as Heppiolette picks himself up off the floor and receives hugs and kisses from his team-mates.

"Preston are proving a point after Fulham's bright start, and are getting better all the time," confirms Davies as a Preston move down the Fulham right forces yet another corner. Clark once more swings the ball in and Lloyd sends a looping header goalbound, only to see Fred Callaghan clear off the line.

It's been a frustrating first half for the home side, and this is encapsulated in an extraordinary swing and connect on Spark's shin by Steve Earle, after a push-and-shove incident near the Preston box. This makes Davies's blood boil. "Whatever was done to Earle you cannot condone players kicking each other like that! A thoroughly stupid action by Earle."

HEPPO, HEPPO, HEPPOLETTE: Winner

Fulham are ending the first half as they began it. Hawkins, that most solid of defenders, clears away the free kick, but the ball is returned with interest, at head height across the six-yard box resulting in "... a great save by Alan Kelly, he really pulled that out of the air and it stuck to his fingertips." There is time for a great shot by George Johnston to be saved by Kelly before half time.

Fulham really turn the screw in the second half. They attack both flanks with swift moves, and it's a ball played in by Barrett on the left that sees Kelly risk life and limb at the feet of the oncoming Johnston. When Johnston is replaced by Vic Halom, the heat is turned up even higher.

Division Three: Fulham 0 Preston North End 1

DATE: May 1, 1971 LENGTH: 60 minutes BROADCASTER: BBC MOTD

CHAMPIONS: Preston's 1970-71 title winners. Back (left to right): David Wilson, George Ross, John McMahon, Ricky Heppolette, Norman Lloyd. Middle: Arthur Cox (coach), Graham Hawkins, John Bird, David Hughes, Gerry Stewart, Alec Spark, Jim McNab, Harry Hubbick (trainer). Front: Bert Patrick, Gerry Ingram, Bobby Ham, Alan Ball senior (manager), Clive Clark, Alan Spavin, George Lyall.

The increasingly menacing Barrett, *now* playing in an apparent free role, tees up Halom 15 yards out, but he shoots wide. Barrett then fires in a great cross for Halom to head just over. There is no respite for Preston as their box is bombarded from all directions.

With just under 15 minutes left, Barrett himself is bearing down on goal and fires in a shot that beats Kelly, only to be cleared off the line by Heppolette. Preston are creaking, and the tension for their fans is unbearable.

A midfield punt from Horne finds Barrett on the left, unmarked as the Preston defence is caught rushing out, leaving Kelly alone at the back. Barrett delivers a superb low cross to Kelly's left for Halom to run onto and surely convert. However he is thwarted by an unbelievable lunging tackle by the classy John Bird that is worthy of saving any game.

After a minute or so of injury time, referee John Gow blows the final whistle and the celebrations begin for the Preston team, management and fans. "Preston have their victory and today we have seen the best two teams in the division," Davies concludes. Preston would go on to beat Rotherham in their final game and be crowned champions.

For Preston, with such a famous past, but starved of 1960s success, (although remarkably they still stand fourth of 140 clubs in the all-time English League table), it was a season to savour. Local North End fan and writer Jon Roper recalls: "I have watched Preston since 1967, seen play-offs, promotions and championships, but that day and that game in West London is the one I will take with me to my grave."

But perhaps the final words should go to then North End skipper Hawkins. After watching the game again, he sent me a text. It simply read: "Fantastic memories."

TV ARCHIVE

WIN OR BUST

CHAPTER 3

1971/72

SPURS V PRESTON NORTH END
PRESTON NORTH END V SPURS
LEAGUE CUP 4TH ROUND OCT 27TH & NOV 8TH 1971

League Cup holders given plenty to think about…

When the draw for the League Cup fourth round was made in early October 1971, North End stood 16th in Division Two with a rather dismal nine points from 11 games. A replay win at home against Watford by 2-1 had ensured that a ball with the Lilywhites number on it was in the velvet bag – and what a plum tie it managed to draw! North End would travel to White Hart Lane to meet Tottenham Hotspur – the holders of the trophy – on October 27th.

In the meantime there were three Division Two fixtures to fulfil, a home fixture against Carlisle United, and away games at Orient and Birmingham City. A decisive win over our Cumbrian friends by 3-0, was followed by a narrow defeat at Orient, North End going down 2-3 but surely heartened in the manner of their performance. A 2-2 draw at St. Andrews against Birmingham City again held out some hopes of an improvement in form, with North End fighting back twice to achieve parity. The second equaliser was prodded home in the dying seconds by debutant Alan Tarbuck, who had arrived at Deepdale for the princely sum of £3,000 after the sale of Bobby Ham to Rotherham United.

In the same period, Spurs had seen off Wolves at home by 4-1, drawn 0-0 away at Nantes in the European Cup Winners Cup and then roundly thrashed Nottingham Forest 6-1 at 'The Lane' just four days before they were due to welcome North End!

And so the build up to the big match in London began, and Preston was buzzing. The Lancashire Evening Post (LEP) ran an interesting piece on match day by the Spurs winger, Ralph Coates in which he highlighted the three main reasons why Spurs would have to be on their guard against Preston that very same night:-

"There are three reasons for our attitude that will close the door on any complacency threatened because Preston are only a Division Two side freshly arrived from Division Three. They are:

1 *Bill Nicholson, our manager, is constantly fighting against such suicidal outlooks in football,*
2 *Spurs remember only too clearly the close game they had against THIRD DIVISION Aston Villa before they finally won their automatic ticket into Europe last season, and...*
3 *Preston are managed by Alan Ball.*

My impression of the two Alan Balls that we all know so well is that the only difference between them is their age, because father and son not only look alike and act alike, they both like to win very much!"

In his preview for the game in the LEP, Norman Shakeshaft sensed that the North End players were very eager to play. Even the fact that Spurs had put six past Forest the previous Saturday was being shrugged off. *"It's Spurs who have every reason to be afraid,"* explained club captain Alan Spavin. *"The pressure will be off us and we will be able to play with real freedom. Man for man they are better, but our team spirit is tremendous."* Ricky Heppolette added, *"We will give them a run for their money – we aren't afraid."*

Ball's rallying cry was the headline however. *"We will return as proud as when we left,"* he promised, and in situations such as these it was impossible for the North End faithful not to believe him.

Just over 30,000 were ready and waiting at White Hart Lane as the teams walked out of the tunnel, which was set into the corner of the main stand.

The Lilywhites lined up with:-

Kelly, McMahon, Ritchie, Bird, Hawkins, Spavin, Heppolette, Ingram, McIlmoyle, Lyall and Clark. Sub: Spark.

The game began true to predictions with the lion's share of the possession belonging to the home side. North End were happy to sit back, bide their time and wait for the opportunities to arise. Their crisp and honest tackling was a feature of the first half, and as Tottenham's initial energy surge subsided, North End started to poke their noses further and further forward.

Ball appeared to have assigned John Bird to take care of the potentially huge threat of England centre forward Martin Chivers, as the two of them wandered everywhere together.

Despite North End packing their box with eight or nine men when under threat, they had survived pretty well in the first half and were a model of efficiency and organisation. The North End midfield was buzzing in a very positive way.

Time and time again they refused to allow the Spurs stars to settle on the ball, bringing ever increasing groans from the home supporters. In fact, during the first half hour Spurs were restricted to just one worthwhile shot – an Alan Mullery 25 yard blast that just cleared the crossbar. Alan Kelly was eventually forced to make his first real save from a Jimmy Pearce drive that had taken a deflection. A few minutes prior to that, Pearce was racing in from the right when John Ritchie hauled him down and was booked for his trouble.

Things changed however in the 40th minute when Jimmy Neighbour took a corner for Spurs on the left. The ball was floated in and Chivers ran back in the direction of his own goal before meeting the ball with a corkscrew twist of his head, sending the ball high into the North End net from around 10 yards, well beyond Kelly's reach.

The second half opened with more of the same as Spurs went for the kill. In the 57th minute, Chivers found a rare couple of yards of space in the penalty area, turned and hit a powerful rising drive that hit the underside of the bar before being hastily cleared.

Ten minutes later it was Chivers again who reached the ball first after a complete miskick in the North End box by Ritchie – the resulting snatched shot going over the bar.

Though Spurs held the lead, as the game entered its last phase they seemed like a team who just wanted the whistle to blow and be content to take the 1-0 win. A fatal state of mind!

In the 85th minute, Alan Spavin played a short corner on the right to Clive Clark, the ball eventually finding George Lyall on the edge of the Spurs box. Collecting the ball with his right foot, he swivelled, took aim and fired in a fierce low left foot shot which beat the agonising dive of Pat Jennings to level the scores.

There was little time left for Spurs – still in a state of shock – to find the speed and train of thought of earlier and pinch a winner. In fact, it was North End who nearly won the game in the final seconds when Gerry Ingram shrugged off a challenge, broke clear and shot narrowly wide with Jennings beaten.

The final whistle blew to loud North End celebrations. Spurs would have to come up north to Deepdale now, meaning another good payday for North End, who were seemingly always desperately short of funds.

Post match, North End were in a happy mood at their London hotel. A businessman supporter had sent them a crate of champagne to celebrate a great performance.

Looking back on the game John Bird commented, *"Martin (Chivers) only got clear of me twice – but he got a goal the first time and hit the crossbar second time!"*

Goal hero George Lyall : *"It was a good time to score. There were only a few minutes to go and they hadn't got the time to get ahead again."*

Alan Spavin : *"We were great weren't we? We matched Spurs in the first half even though they took the lead and we really sickened them by equalising at the end. I have never known North End have so much fighting spirit as we have now."*

Of course, the last word to goes to manager Alan Ball. *"I said that we would be proud and we are proud. This is our night on the town and don't we deserve it!"*

QUOTE

—Alan Ball

—Alan Spavin

PRESTON BRING HOME LONDON PRIDE

PRESTON manager Alan Ball was so delighted last night that he even sang a couple of songs for ...

The replay was to take place a week later than planned on Monday 8th November, as Spurs had to fulfill the second leg of their clash with

Nantes on the originally scheduled League Cup date.

Over the next few days, North End far from celebrating became dismayed about the bias against them in some newspaper reports of the southern editions of the nationals following their draw at White Hart Lane.

So much so, that even the North End official programme 'Club Notes' feature for the Division Two game against Hull City on October 30th, growled out loud :-

"For some obscure reason it (the performance) *received grudged and scanty praise, as if giving any had the taste of sour grapes. Surely the most biased critic could see some merit in such an achievement?*

"If the team had gone to White Hart Lane feeling what the vast majority of people thought about their chances of averting defeat, they may as well have stayed at home or accepted the seemingly inevitable. Tottenham, League Cup holders, after all were unbeaten on their own ground, having won six and drawn one of seven league matches by 21 goals to four, with a 6-1 win their most recent proof of their power.

"Alan Ball had other ideas. He promised we would be proud of the team and was right because he put his own unquenchable spirit into the team. The late equaliser was earned by fighting to the finish."

I have found one such match report during my research. The reporter – a massive football 'name' on Fleet Street at the time, as well as a Spurs fan and Jimmy Greaves idoliser – ploughed into North End's performance from start to finish. It begins right from the opening paragraph and the insults just carry on: *"Preston last night proved to Tottenham that they who run away really do live to fight another day."*

"Preston's triumph last night was a defeat for football"

"This carefully planned lock-out by Preston manager Alan Ball was a totally boring success"

However, the credibility of the ranting report is somewhat scuppered by a post-match quote from Spurs manager Bill Nicholson at the end of the article. *"We didn't play well and are disappointed that we have to replay. If I had been the Preston manager I would have been very pleased with the way they played."*

What we learned from all that was that Bill Nicholson understood football! Alan Ball meanwhile was not letting it drop and devoted most of his weekly LEP *Football Post* column to the subject.

He went through countless accusations and answered them all before declaring he preferred to believe the evidence of his own eyes and the comments of the Spurs manager and chairman.

"Bill Nicholson came up to me in the boardroom afterwards and said, "Preston played well and you should be proud of your team. Congratulations." The Tottenham chairman then said he thought it had been a great game, and added what a great battle we had put up."

Amidst all the fall-out from that game, North End continued their good form and beat Hull City at home 3-1 and then went one better by travelling to Ayresome Park and nicking a 1-0 win against Middlesbrough.

And so to the replay… could North End do it?!

Alan Ball's passionate message for the fans on match day was just what was needed. *"We will give everything we have got tonight – and more besides. If that isn't enough to bring a win, all I can say is that we will have done everything we possibly could. By God, we will have a real go!"*

I was in the fourth year at secondary school at that time, a very important year as we worked towards our final exams a year later. Having been so easily led away from all things educational in the previous year by North End's promotion campaign, a few words of 'friendly' advice had found their way into my ear from a couple of teachers before we broke for the summer holiday. I had heeded their advice and was well back on track with my studies by now. The school I attended was 'strict discipline' with a liberal sprinkling of corporal punishment, which I'm sure would horrify the youth of today.

I remember pushing my luck with one of them, the Geography teacher (a known football fan) before a double lesson, asking him if we could postpone homework just this once so that I could go and watch the big match. This was the last subject of the day and so far, no homework received that needed to be in by the following day. A resounding 'NO' coupled with a look of *'the temerity of it'* saw me slope off toward my seat. I tried again. "Sir, I bet if you were me and it was Everton who were playing Spurs in the cup, you wouldn't want any homework..." Eyes raised to the heavens, he didn't respond.

The end of the lesson duly arrived, and he told us what was required for homework. Just as my heart was sinking he said, "So who of you besides Skingsley are hoping to go and watch the football tonight?" I hardly dare look up! Wow, he was actually considering putting the homework on the back burner! A quick count saw about half the class put their hand up, all boys.

"Well I want your best efforts on this homework because it's going towards your project marks..." Oh no...NO...he's going to make us do it, I remember thinking. He continued "...so, as it won't be fair on the girls, make sure that you all hand it in on Wednesday morning...ok?"

Lots of smiles as the class exited and made the way towards the cloakrooms and then off home.

I thanked the teacher, and he just smiled and said, "Think they'll win?" I told him I wasn't sure but loved being there when there was a big crowd. "Enjoy it...but remember I want that work in for Wednesday. It's counting towards your mock result." Top man!

Deepdale was heaving when I finally got onto the West Paddock. There were people and queues everywhere outside the ground, and I had left home 45 minutes earlier than usual.

Although it was quite breezy, there was the usual smell that prevailed at Deepdale on well attended night matches – a heady mixture of cigarette smoke, Bovril and alcohol – as we waited for the teams to emerge. There was always a five second warning that the teams were about to enter the arena, as North End's then signature tune would begin.

The big drums would belt out the beat of the first few bars of James Last's version of *'March of the Toreadors'* from the opera *'Carmen'* over the tannoy system and every North End fans head would turn towards the tunnel ready to applaud the team on to the pitch.

North End fielded:-

Kelly, McMahon, Ritchie, Bird, Hawkins, Spavin, Heppolette, Clark, McIlmoyle, Lyall and Ingram. Sub: Spark

Spurs, in a delightful ensemble of pale yellow shirts with matching socks complemented with white shorts, looked like a well oiled machine in the first few minutes following the kick-off. I could immediately tell that this team was far above the usual standard of the 'Division Two true grit' that usually adorned Deepdale. They seemed to glide around, move quickly and pass very accurately.

In the third minute, North End used up one of their 'lives' when Alan Gilzean's back header was perfectly placed and left Martin Chivers in the clear with just Alan Kelly to beat. There was a collective holding of breath from the huge crowd, but Chivers slashed his shot wide of the post and we breathed again. North End got their act together so well in defence after that escape that it was Spurs' last sight of Kelly for over half an hour.

During this time, North End harried, bustled and hustled non-stop, though chances were very few and far between. Roared on by their huge support whenever in possession, they kept driving forward.

A cross from John McMahon was launched into the Spurs penalty area and caused some panic as the visitors could not clear their lines, following Ray Evans' initial attempt to clear – his header travelling skywards. The ball bobbed about around the six yard box as screams of anticipation were screeched from the crowd. Ricky Heppolette finally hurled himself at the ball and his header fizzed just over the bar.

The next time the crowd were tantalised by North End it was George Lyall providing the drama. Homing in towards the Spurs box, he cheekily beat Steve Perryman one way, then the other, then side stepped Martin Peters. Pushing the ball forward with one last touch, he launched a superb drive past the scrambling Pat Jennings and sadly, just past the post. More roars of approval for North End, who were certainly trying to make things happen for their fans.

Spurs then finally revisited the North End box, as Chivers and John Pratt revealed their class in a delicate passing movement that placed Pratt 10 yards out with just Kelly to beat. Fortunately, for North End at least, Pratt lost his footing in the act of shooting and ballooned his effort high and wide.

Half time arrived and North End left the field to rapturous applause.

In those days, there was no segregation of fans and there were many Spurs fans in the West Paddock enjoying the game. On that night at least, there was never a hint of trouble.

Within a few minutes of the restart, Chivers was booked for dissent after failing to retreat 10 yards at a free kick. Very soon he was in action again smoothly proceeding into the North End penalty area and passing sideways for Gilzean, who had to settle for a corner as his mishit shot caught McMahon's leg on its way to the byline.

North End eventually got themselves together again and resumed their assault. It was McMahon who next drew loud applause from the crowd with a trademark shot on the run from the corner of the Spurs box. With boot meeting ball perfectly, it drew a save from Pat Jennings that made the crowd gasp. Arrowing rapidly towards the top corner, the ball was palmed away one handed by the Northern Ireland international goalkeeper's fantastic trademark backwards leap, which drew loud appreciation from fans of both teams.

On the game went, and with just six minutes to go that man Chivers broke the deadlock. A seemingly harmless punt forward by Spurs left back Cyril Knowles saw the England striker chest the ball down, take three strides forward, leaving John Bird behind and facing Alan Kelly to drive a low shot past the Republic of Ireland goalkeeper's outstretched right hand from just inside the penalty area. It was rough justice for Bird as he had policed perhaps Europe's best striker well up to that point.

Only the Spurs fans jumped up and down this time, but as Hugh McIlmoyle kicked off again at the restart, little did we know he was about to raise the Deepdale roof!

McIlmoyle had been signed in the close season from Middlesbrough, and was a real football 'nomad'. North End were his seventh club, and everywhere he had lathered Dubbin on his boots he had scored goals. Indeed at this point in the season, the second week in November, he was the Lilywhites leading scorer with nine goals.

Up to this point, he had been contained supremely well by Spurs' Welsh international centre half Mike England, but as North End launched a fantastic last salvo at the Spurs goal, McIlmoyle's scoring instinct was about to kick in.

Just three minutes were left on the clock when the ball bounced out on the right for a North End corner. With manager Ball out of the dugout waving his arms to urge every North End player bar Kelly forward, Alan Spavin placed the ball and floated it into the danger zone.

The delivery was perfect. The ball was met by Bird whose high leap flicked the ball quickly and downwards towards the six yard box. Time seemed to default to slow motion as McIlmoyle thrust himself forward from the right post area, diving amongst the feet of a cluster of four Spurs defenders to head the ball home from no more than three yards. It was a sensational goal. His bravery drew just reward, and the accompanying thunderous roar signalled it was game-on again!

However, with just a minute left and whistles from the crowd being heard, suddenly from absolutely nowhere Martin Peters was bearing down on the North End goal with just Kelly in his path. This was Peters' supreme talent. His positional sense and anticipation were exceptional. With loud screams of panic coming from the home fans, John McMahon, haring after the England international, threw himself into a sliding tackle that was both valiant and painful, but above all else successful.

Hugh McIlmoyle (on floor, nearest to goal), sees his diving header cross the line

This match had been just wonderful, and when the referee blew for full time the crowd showed their appreciation, long and loud.

A few North End players were being treated for cramp and looked exhausted whilst listening to Ball on the pitch near the players' tunnel in the few minutes before extra time commenced. Spurs looked a little more relaxed as Bill Nicholson spoke to his players on a more individual basis.

The match resumed, and from somewhere – maybe the words of Ball – North End summoned still more endeavour and were the better side. The game had become end-to-end in the search for another goal that would surely prove fatal for the opposition. The second period commenced, and on 113 minutes it was finally decided.

The now increasingly leg weary Preston ranks lost concentration as Steve Perryman engineered a break by passing a through ball to Jimmy Neighbour. Perryman carried on his run to meet Neighbour's perfectly placed right wing cross flush on his head to send the ball speeding past Kelly's despairing dive and effectively heave the holders over a very formidable Preston North End barrier.

The final whistle blew and the gratitude of the fans resounded stridently. It's always disappointing to lose, but North End had been superb – and it wasn't just the fans who said it.

THE BIG MATCH

Preston play their hearts out

"REMEMBER their centre forward is probably worth more than my entire team . . . At least we did not lose as heavily as Everton did on Saturday." Preston boss ALAN BALL.

"PRESTON were a hard side to beat but we should have done better. We did not play well, particularly in the first half."—Spurs boss BILL NICHOLSON

STEVE PERRYMAN

THE AGE OF MIRACLES IS PAST!

WELL, the miracle did not happen. Preston could not beat mighty Tottenham Hotspur to go through to the fifth round of the League Cup, but, as North End manager Alan Ball promised, the players gave everything they had got and more besides.

There was no disgrace in the Second Division side losing 2-1 to the trophy holders after extra time and every Preston supporter in the crowd of 27,239 had reason to hold his head high.

[illegible]

North End's moment of glory as Hugh McIlmoyle dives to head the equaliser in a packed goalmouth.

There were congratulations on North End's effort from Bill Nicholson and Jock Stein, who had been watching from the Pavilion Stand. He had been particularly impressed with Lyall, but in truth North End had 11 heroes that night.

Ball was concerned that the North End fans, despite a magnificent showing, had ultimately witnessed their team being beaten again. *"I desperately wanted for us to win that match for them so they could have something to shout about and feel proud."* He added, *"Maybe I should have used different tactics – but at least we didn't go down as heavily as Everton did against Spurs last weekend when they lost 3-0. My son told me they would murder us, but they didn't did they?!"*

Remarkably, Chivers played for England v Switzerland on the following evening at Wembley, albeit as a substitute after his Deepdale endeavours. Peters was also in the squad, but was rested.

North End lost to Spurs by the odd goal in five over 210 minutes. The fans had every reason to feel proud of their team. Blackpool, waiting in the wings for the winner, duly went down 2-0 at White Hart Lane nine days later.

Graham Hawkins takes an elbow to the face as Pat Jennings punches away a corner from Alan Spavin

Top: Steve Perryman(next to post) heads the ball toward the North End goal...
Bottom: ...and sees the ball beat Alan Kelly's despairing dive for the winner

Courtesy Bob Bond

No computers or mobile phones for kids to fiddle around with back in the 70's –they read comics, and sometimes they contained a feature about one of their hero's!

CHAPTER 4

1971/72

PRESTON NORTH END V MILLWALL
DECEMBER 11TH 1971

The complete and utter taming of the Lions...

Of all the matches that I have ever watched, this is the one to which I always mentally return to when discussions over a pint arise and you are asked as to where and when was the best North End performance in your lifetime?

North End's memorable run since early October 1971 (see next page) was now looking rather impressive. Something had obviously changed since the early season 'hit and miss' form, and confidence was coursing through the team as the list of successes was added to weekly.

This period was surely the peak of Alan Ball's powers at Deepdale. His team were playing some wonderful and entertaining football that – as I pointed out above – will live in the memory bank forever.

"That run was as good as it got for us back then. We were not worried about anybody. The two games against Spurs had come in the middle of

the run and despite just missing out it actually bolstered us – we really worried them and they were a big expensive team even back then. The crowd backed us and roared us on and we wanted to perform for them," Graham Hawkins told me few years ago when we met up for a 'little chat' that lasted all afternoon...

06/10/71	Watford v Preston North End	D	1-1	LC
09/10/71	Portsmouth v Preston North End	D	1-1	D2
11/10/71	Preston North End v Watford	W	2-1	LC
16/10/71	Preston North End v Carlisle United	W	3-0	D2
18/10/71	Orient v Preston North End	L	3-2	D2
23/10/71	Birmingham City v Preston North End	D	2-2	D2
27/10/71	Tottenham H v Preston North End	D	1-1	LC
30/10/71	Preston North End v Hull City	W	3-1	D2
06/11/71	Middlesbrough v Preston North End	W	0-1	D2
08/11/71	Preston North End v Tottenham H	L	1-2	LC
13/11/71	Preston North End v Sheffield Wed	W	1-0	D2
20/11/71	Swindon Town v Preston North End	D	1-1	D2
27/11/71	Preston North End v Watford	W	2-0	D2
04/12/71	Blackpool v Preston North End	D	1-1	D2

On December 11th 1971, North End were hosting Millwall. They sat in second place in Division Two with 29 points; Norwich City led with 31. North End were a creditable eighth since embarking on their great autumn run, with a tally of 22 points. They had taken a point away from Bloomfield Road the previous week with a late goal by Clive Clark, and came into this match determined to puncture Millwall's balloon.

Mind you, none of this was really in my mind as I wandered down Skeffington Road that day. I was more concerned with avoiding the freezing cold wind with occasional matching rain. Over the recent weeks I had migrated to the Town End – towards the top left when viewed from the Kop – to avoid weather like this particular day...after all I was the grand old age of 14 back then!

There were regulars who stood around there and I enjoyed listening to their comments, often suppressing the urge to laugh out loudly. They were real characters one and all.

There was a bloke who had obviously been working on Saturday morning if his clothes were anything to go by, who smoked a lot and was very demonstrative; always showing the player he was moaning about how he should have taken the free kick or saved the ball, by swinging his leg in a particular way or leaping high off his feet, miming catching and hugging the ball. Others too, who would voice their immediate and serious opinions loudly causing so much local laughter that they laughed at themselves too in the end! I would often replay these comments in my mind at home later in the evening, randomly smiling or laughing out while eating my tea or watching television. I just used to explain by saying it was something I had heard at North End that afternoon.

There was one other duo always there too, a bloke approaching his 50's and his dad - well into his 70's. Their relationship was hilarious; the son was like the rest of the spectators there, enthralled and moved to shout now and again. Dad was a big bloke, unsteady on his feet and took an age to navigate the steps up to the back of the Town End. He always had to be assisted by his son whenever moving around.

Having scaled the steps to the shelter at the back of the Town End on this particular day, the informal nods of recognition to the usual friendly faces commenced. It was just after this that John (the son) revealed to one and all that his dad (Alf) had been put on water tablets by the doctor a few days previously and had become 'a bloody waterfall' and since then, life had become 'a bloody nightmare at our house.'

I was looking at my feet suppressing laughter at this point.

"He didn't want to come on...did yer?" he said turning to his dad. He continued, "but my mum said he had to. She said she's up to here with it. God only knows how this lot will pan out here this afternoon. "

Keeping my head down I was biting my lip now and pretending to read the programme.

I was usually in position by 2:30pm, and on this very chilly day, a half decent crowd of just over 14,000 braved the conditions to see if North End could upset the Millwall apple cart.

The teams duly ran out, North End in their usual white and blue garb, Millwall in light yellow shirts and white shorts – replicating the Spurs away kit seen at Deepdale a few weeks previously.

It was obvious from watching the kick-in that Hugh McIlmoyle and Ricky Heppolette had failed their morning fitness tests, so Ball went with:-

Kelly, McMahon, Ritchie, Bird, Hawkins, Spavin, Spark, Clark, Tarbuck, Lyall, Ingram. Sub : McNab

There was a real buzz about the crowd. North End hadn't lost in the league for nigh on two months and were in great form. If they could do a job on the Londoners it would lift their reputation a little further, just about everywhere.

The match kicked off...and just a few seconds in I heard John behind me, "Oh bloody hell, here we go. You're bloody joking dad."

"I can't bloody help it! Grab my hand and get me t'bloody toilet quick." Much nattering from John, but off they set on their sojourn to the toilets, each Town End step taken one by one...slowly.

An early raid into the North End box came to nothing with Derek Possee firing well wide and into the well populated Kop which prompted North End to slip into gear.

When Alan Spavin and George Lyall started spraying 25 yard passes to feet from midfield you just knew this was going to be another good day.

And boy, was this going to be a good day!

Lyall was first to break from the confines of midfield. Wandering past four Millwall players using his pace and guile, this early run produced a snap shot from the edge of the box that in the event flew harmlessly wide. That was his sighter.

After just 12 minutes North End took the lead. Clive Clark was bowled over on the left, and left back John Ritchie strode forward to place the ball. He delivered a lovely curling ball; coming towards goalkeeper Bryan King and then leaving him. He could only push the ball away to the right where John McMahon was waiting, all alone.

Steadying himself, the big right back sent a cross back into the danger area enabling the wholehearted Alan Tarbuck to find the net with a neat twisting header. This was Tarbuck's fourth goal in the five games he had started since being snapped up by Ball from Chester City.

Alan Tarbuck (extreme left, partially hidden), arrows his header between defender and goalkeeper to open the scoring for North End

As North End walked back to take their places for the restart, a gradually intensifying roar went around the ground, to the point of deafening as Millwall tapped the ball forward. It really was appreciation from the North End faithful and in the only way they knew how, were asking for more.

Looking around during the crowd celebrations just after the ball nestled in the net, I noted that John and Alf still weren't back and felt sorry that they'd missed out. I looked down at the bottom right hand corner and there they were – preparing to scale Alf's very own 'Annapurna'. Well at least they were on their way back now...

The visitors almost cashed in shortly afterwards. Inexplicably, Ritchie passed the ball straight to Derek Smethurst, with Alan Kelly hopelessly out of position. Snatching at the chance, the ex-Chelsea forward found the Kop about 40 rows up from the edge of the box.

It was North End who were catching the eye though, with Spavin and Lyall almost taunting their immediate (and notable) opponents Gordon Bolland and Eamonn Dunphy, as they upped the tempo. Spavin was now prominent, and split the visitors defence in two with a pass of sublime quality into the path of the ever willing Alex Spark; the on-the-run drive going narrowly wide.

Just after the speedy Tarbuck had all but intercepted a nonchalant Millwall back-pass, it was Lyall's turn to demonstrate the art of launching a killer pass. Clark, haring in from the left touchline gratefully controlled the ball on the move and manufactured a delightful curling lob that was just a couple of inches wide of the top corner with King stranded on the six yard line.

The crowd were loving it, and roaring North End on. The players were responding, it was like Division One playing Division Four in terms of quality.

Spavin and Lyall combined to walk through the Millwall midfield and press forward themselves. After some superb edge of the box intricacies from 'Spav' he neatly tapped the ball sideways enabling the eager Lyall to launch one of his 'specials' at the Millwall goal. The fierce drive was superbly palmed away for a corner by King at his full extent.

More crowd roaring, more crowd approval.

A hopeful punt forward by Bolland found Ritchie, but the North End full back stumbled and Possee gained possession. Graham Hawkins involved himself quickly, blocking Possee's path with a strong tackle and walking away with the ball while the Millwall forward picked himself up off the floor.

Alf and John were back by this point, as John barked out his usual praise for Hawkins, "G'lad Lerch!" always followed by a few sentences as to why Hawkins was one of the best buys North End ever made. It was hard to disagree!

Play switched quickly to the Millwall end, Spark teeing up Lyall for another on-target pile driver that King gathered after his initial parry.

It was noticeable how McMahon was moving forward and playing on the right side of midfield at every opportunity. This left just Ritchie, Bird and Hawkins at the back, but they seemed to be coping admirably. Ball's tactics were swamping the Millwall midfield, and in effect negating it. They were always it seemed, trailing behind the North End players.

Spark blasted in a shot from 20 yards and saw his effort, screaming towards the bottom corner, turned away by King at the very last instant. Spavin then tried his luck, dispatching a low, humming drive, a constant six inches off the surface towards King's bottom right. King once more excelled himself by pushing the shot past his post.

This was wonderful to watch; a joy that I will never forget it!

Pressure and more pressure! North End would not let up. Gerry Ingram who had concerned himself in the main to neat flicks, laying the ball off and taking the brunt of the huge Millwall centre half Barry Kitchener in his stride, was next to have a try at securing the second goal. A sparkling Clark run down the left resulted in a fine cross that saw Ingram leap high and direct a firm header just wide.

More clapping, banging of feet and screaming of "come on" as King placed the ball for the goal kick. The crowd atmosphere, like the North End performance, was quite fantastic.

I know from the timings it must have been around now when I heard John say, "Oh bloody hell. Already? We missed the first 'un, can't you hang on till half time Dad?"

"No."

And so it was that off they trotted at a snail's pace to the toilet behind the Town End.

From the goal kick, Spark headed the ball to Spavin, Spavin passed to Lyall, Lyall placed the ball directly into McMahon's path powering down the right wing. Teeing himself up on the fly, the right back hammered in the most wonderful rising shot that beat everything and everybody in its flight path – including the formidable King. As the screams of expectation in the crowd peaked, the ball smashed into the angle of post and bar and ballooned high into the Town End.

More deafening crowd appreciation and in my mind's eye I can see a Millwall player on his haunches looking at King and shaking his head. The goal frame was still wobbling as King placed the ball for the goal kick.

How much longer could Millwall scrape by???

The answer was...not very long.

Kitchener couldn't quite keep up with Ingram who had read Lyall's threaded ball into the box perfectly and manhandled the centre forward with enough intent to satisfy the referee it was a penalty.

Ingram wasn't flustered and coolly stroked the penalty home to unbounded glee from the home fans. What a noise!

There was around five minutes left of the first half still to go, which

North End closed out tremendously well. Indeed, the half ended with Lyall demonstrating supreme and cheeky confidence. He had received the ball a few seconds before the half time whistle blew and must have noticed the ref out of the corner of his eye. He then proceeded to perform 'keepy uppy' in front of the Millwall midfielders before catching the ball as the whistle sounded, politely handing it to the ref!

North End walked off to a half time standing ovation, after destroying a 'promotion favourite.' What would the second half bring?

The crowd were buoyant at half time, genuinely excited at the quality of

Gerry Ingram calmly sends the Millwall 'keeper the wrong way from the penalty spot

the North End performance. It was during the interval, whilst having a drink of coffee from my flask (thanks mum!) that Alf and John returned.

"Did you see the second goal?" someone asked. "Did I hell. We had just started back and someone shouted 'it's a North End pen' so I propped Dad against t'toilet wall and told him not to move. I ran back toward t'corner down there but give up when I heard t'cheer."

Poor John, he sounded really depressed. Alf didn't look happy either!

The second half commenced with the North End fans in good heart, and was obvious that the visitors had been 'spoken to' by their manager, Benny Fenton.

North End were being tested a little more than in the first half, and had to be on their toes on the hour mark when Possee was put through into 'apparent' space by a Bolland pass near the North End box.

I say 'apparent' because it was an illiusion from my vantage point. Within milliseconds Hawkins and John Bird had performed a pincer movement that General Montgomery would have been proud of, relieving the diminutive striker of the ball and driving North End forward again.

From the moment Spavin collected the ball, it signalled all sorts of forward movement by North End.

As Tarbuck peeled away and started running towards the right wing, Spark started a run towards the box. Clark began to move in from the left wing too as Spavin curled a 10 yard pass across the middle for Lyall to run on to. The glorious 25 yard pass to Tarbuck that Lyall executed brought gasps from the crowd, as all the little striker had to do was take a steadying touch in his stride and cross the ball to the Spark, arriving bang on cue into the penalty area.

This was done perfectly; Spark's near post run was made without a defender in sight and the reliable Scot met the ball without flaw, flicking the ball onwards and straight behind for Clark to power home a header on the run from a couple of yards out. Millwall had been stripped bare. It was sheer delightful football from North End!

Delight too from John and Alf – their first goal of the afternoon – but what a brilliant one to witness!

Off all my years of watching North End, I had never known the crowd so happy and content. North End were not only winning games, but were playing with such style, finesse and purpose that their belief in Ball and themselves was unbounded. It was no surprise that the crowd was screaming, "Alan Ball, Alan Ball, Alan Ball….." for quite a while afterwards. In the 18 months he had been at Deepdale, he had taken the club out of Division Three and to the top end of Division Two.

The game settled down a little after the Clark goal, but it was still North End dominating in all areas. A snap shot on the turn from Tarbuck went just wide and so did a diving header from Ingram following a Clark centre. Meanwhile at the other end Possee hadn't given up yet, firing in a couple of low shots that Kelly collected easily. Lyall moved forward again, looked up and fired in a cannonball shot that just went wide of the goal.

Clive Clark heads home North End's third goal following superb teamwork

It was noticeable that the crowd were not leaving their places, despite the big North End gates which must have been open for about 10 minutes at least by this point. Certainly a first in my experience!

There were a couple of people on the move again however – Alf and

John. A combination of water tablets, cold weather and excitement had seen to it that another visit to the toilets was necessary straight away. I remember the look John gave us as he dutifully followed and steadied his dad on the terracing. A half smile, raised eyes and a shake of the head. Good people, both. That was the last I saw of them that day.

McMahon, who had played a sterling role on the right, supplementing the midfield when necessary, was booked for handball with just minutes to go. It was to be the only blot on the copybook for North End, but as it turned out there was still time for them to construct yet another goal to compensate for this indiscretion.

George Lyall hammers home the fourth goal (top) and is congratulated by his teammates (centre, bottom)

It was a strike that truly crowned a marvelous display. Breaking free from midfield and running through the now dispirited Millwall defence, Lyall exchanged passes with Clark who had tracked his teammates run.

The wingers' return pass was perfect and found 'Sugar' Lyall in the perfect place to launch his final missile of the day at the Millwall goal. King dived to his right but the shot had too much on it and gave him no chance.

I can still see the fans on the Kop now jumping around in delirium as King dragged himself up off the floor to retrieve the ball from the back right hand corner of his net. A couple of minutes later, the final whistle blew. Another first for me at this point, as I witnessed the crowd roaring, shouting, singing and applauding their approval of this quite stunning North End display. There was even a crowd invasion of sorts by the younger fans eager to thank their heroes with a pat on the back.

Football Post

MAC AND HIS BOSS TO FACE THE FA

My weekend of worry

Gold Cup victory for Leap Frog

SUPERB PNE TAME LIONS!

Scoreboard

'Winning Post' has

A great read to welcome you home on a cold winters night!

This was without doubt Lyall's greatest ever game for North End. He had showcased his full range of skills and demonstrated just what he was capable of. And yet, my abiding memory is of Spavin. The unflappable, cultured, puller of the midfield strings...the imperious Spavin. The word 'imperious' can bring back many definitions depending on your dictionary publisher or web search engine, the one that I found best was *'of the emperor'*. Spavin was certainly the 'Emperor of Deepdale' that day.

I'm pleased to confirm that I didn't dream or overstate any of this either. Norman Shakeshaft who watched, reported and often criticised North End on issues for many years in the *LEP*, had the weekend to reflect on matters and wrote in his column on Monday, December 13th 1971: *"...but for once he (Ball) didn't have to say anything. His players had done it all for him on the field! What a show they put up. I wrote immediately after the game that Preston's performance was their best for years, and on reflection I still cannot withdraw that statement.*

Indeed if anything, it was selling North End short for I have never seen them play better, and bearing in mind the fact that football is faster now with teams employing much more method and tactical skill, I must rate this display as the best ever.

This may sound like sacrilege to those supporters who remember the Finney era and the 30's Cup winning side, but all I can do is agree with Ball who commented that the 14,011 fans present on Saturday were "lucky people."

Millwall had been dismantled first, and then destroyed; their goal peppered with long range missiles and close range fire from a non-stop Preston team. From my perspective, I had never seen before – nor have I since – anything of such sustained control from my home town team. Every North End player was oozing confidence and on the top of their game that particular day; the ultimate 'team machine.'

The 'Football Post' mailbag was swelled to double size in the December 18th issue. Letters, both short and long, paid due homage to the North End victory the previous week.

"Magnificent, tremendous, fantastic was Preston's performance against Millwall..."

"...the team is playing with tremendous confidence; their spirit is sky high..."

"...it was a magnificent team effort, the finest I have ever seen at Deepdale."

" ...and Lyall looked the complete player with his midfield artistry and power shooting. What better tutelage can there be than playing from under the wing of Spavin?"

The win catapulted North End to a worthy fourth position in Division Two. It didn't get any better than this, unfortunately. There was more interest still to come at Deepdale in the FA Cup at least this particular season, but league form nosedived and unbelievably relegation back to Division Three was a real possibility for some time.

Gerry Ingram takes another buffeting from goalkeeper Bryan King and Barry Kitchener

CHAPTER 5

1971/72

PRESTON NORTH END V BRISTOL CITY
FA CUP 3RD ROUND, JANUARY 15TH 1972

Seven incredible minutes...

It was after the Millwall game that North End's form started to wane. Three of the next four league games were lost; the only win being at home to Bristol City on December 27th 1971 in front of a large holiday crowd of almost 20,000.

Coincidentally, North End had been drawn at home to The Robins in the third round of the FA Cup on January 15th, and this was to prove a match with much more of a twist to it than the 1-0 league win.

Another dull, grey and damp Lancashire day provided the setting for the game. Alan Spavin and Gerry Ingram had passed their morning fitness tests, and North End lined up: -

Kelly, McMahon, McNab, Bird, Hawkins, Spavin, Heppolette, Clark, McIlmoyle, Lyall, Ingram. Sub: Lamb

North End began brightly, and in the seventh minute, George Lyall crafted a through ball for Clive Clark to run on to, only for the City goalkeeper, Mike Gibson, to run out from his line and get to the bouncing ball first.

Following an easy save by Alan Kelly after a City free kick, the ball was played down the right by Spavin for John McMahon to run towards, and his blistering drive had Gibson at full stretch tipping the ball away for a corner.

Spavin floated the corner in and it created some havoc in the City goalmouth as a game of head tennis ensued between the respective teams before veteran defender Ken Wimshurst booted the ball well clear of the danger area. Another of City's veterans, centre half Dick Rooks, then floored Clark as he made swift progress down the left wing. After a lecture from the referee, the free kick was taken, but collected with ease by Gibson.

A cross field ball from Spavin was headed on by Gerry Ingram straight into the path of the busy Ricky Heppolette whose cross forced Brian Drysdale into making a hurried clearance. Heppolette was drawing regular applause for his foraging work in midfield, alongside Lyall and Spavin who were also being joined regularly by McMahon, as in the Millwall game a few weeks previously.

It was all Preston, and Lyall almost opened the scoring when he powered in a header from a Clark centre that Geoff Merrick headed off the City line with Gibson already beaten.

Rooks had obviously decided to play the role of 'pantomime villain' for the Deepdale faithful, pushing and barging players regularly when the refs back was turned. He had certainly struck a chord with the Town End fans around my vantage point, and John and his dad, Alf in particular. At one point Alf nearly fell forward from the top step as he started shouting at the ref to sort Rooks out. This caused some consternation, and John bellowed out, "Bloody hell dad, yer nearly went o'er then.

Wind yer bloody neck in!" Alf wasn't having it. "He's just pushed 'Macimoy' (meaning McIlmoyle) face down in't bloody mud and ref's doin' nowt. Useless bugger."

The first 20 minutes had passed and all seemed to be going well. City had barely been out of their half and North End had been on the attack, albeit with nothing to show yet for their efforts.

After 25 minutes, the first wheel fell off the Preston charabanc. The words 'knife' and 'butter' spring to mind as City winger Trevor Tainton flicked the ball infield to Gerry Gow. It looked as though Lyall had the midfielders cross to the far post covered, but he failed to clear the ball and left Peter Spiring with the simple task of firing the ball past an exposed Alan Kelly.

Peter Spiring fires past the helpless Alan Kelly to put Bristol City ahead

It was a dreadful error and there were shouts of disapproval from the crowd. This seemed to be a re-run of the previous home game against Luton Town, where North End had displayed all the enterprise but handed the visitors the points by conceding a soft goal.

Ingram bustled down the left and fired in a cross that Clark scooped just over the bar. With ten minutes left before half time, North End finally equalised. Poetically, it was the ever unpopular Rooks who set North

End's equaliser in motion.

Rooks shanked his attempted clearance straight to Spavin just beyond the City box. After cleverly beating two defenders, he looked up and floated a centre towards the far side of the penalty area where the dropping ball was met full blast by Lyall's right boot and transferred with such velocity into the City net that Gibson was left groping at thin air. There must have surely been a sense of atonement for Lyall after his defensive error.

This time the crowd delivered a tremendous roar of approval, and with this backing, North End intensified their efforts. A Clark free kick, delivered beautifully and at pace directly into Gibson's goalmouth caused untold panic; eventually Jim McNab poking the ball over the bar.

However, North End's new found vigour was short lived as just four minutes after equalising, their absent defence handed City the lead. Tainton's corner was headed home by Les Wilson who rose totally unchallenged to pick his spot from 10 yards. This invited bitter murmurings of discontent from the crowd about North End statues masquerading as defenders.

North End got back on the horse and laid siege to the Bristol City goal once more. Good interplay between Ingram and Hugh McIlmoyle saw Ingram's header go just wide. Heppolette then performed a little piece of magic but saw his exquisite lob from the edge of the box cleared off the line by Drysdale.

With half time all but upon us, John Galley had the Preston fans hardly daring to watch as he picked up a loose ball and fired in a shot that trickled just wide of the post, with Kelly once again left helpless by an absentee defence.

The second half began as the first had ended, with Galley almost scoring after taking advantage of lackadaisical North End defending – this time John Bird letting the ball run free in the area, seemingly unaware that Galley was behind him. Galley was positioning himself when Bird regained his senses and put the ball out for a corner with a slide tackle.

Preston finally got on their feet again and started to dominate. Yet another melee occurred in the City area following a Clark corner but any hopes of an equaliser were dashed when the ref blew for a foul ...on Rooks. This brought another fiery outburst from Alf which yet again had to be doused by his son, John. There was laughter all around as Alf, full of ire following the ref's decision could hardly make himself understood.

To make matters worse, from the free kick Spiring almost latched onto a dreadful North End back pass intended for Kelly after the City move broke down – the Irishman having to run out of his area to fly kick the ball away.

Ingram headed wide from a free kick, and McMahon then tried a long range shot only for Gibson to save easily. The action then swung to the other end as City gained three corners in rapid succession before Graham Hawkins mercilessly put his boot through the ball and cleared North End's lines once and for all.

An injury to Rooks that required the trainer's attention brought a short interlude of merriment from Alf... "Gerrup y'soft bugger"... before the stocky defender jumped to his feet in a sprightly fashion to continue the battle and invite more abuse from the North End diehards. In no time at all Rooks was being spoken to again for clattering through the back of Ingram. That was a cue for more bellowing from Alf and fellow diehards, with the aforementioned Rooks trotting back no doubt smiling to himself.

Once again North End got their heads down and launched assault after assault on the Bristol City goal. Spavin floated a centre into the City box that resulted in a scrum of players anxiously swinging away with their legs and missing the ball. It was a City boot that finally hoofed the ball clear but only as far as Lyall who sent Clark racing away down the left. The flying winger got in a superb cross that McIlmoyle headed just wide.

North End threw everything forward, leaving just Kelly and two other defenders in their own half. City meanwhile had all their men in their own half, and most of them quite often in their own box.

Despite North End's intent, the lack of a breakthrough was causing some degree of barracking from the home supporters but this was switched towards the phlegmatic Rooks when he was substituted around this time. Suddenly developing a very unhealthy limp, he took an eternity to leave the field as the booing and catcalls got ever louder. As he crossed the touchline he turned and clapped each side of the ground, immediately seemed to lose the limp and went to sit in the visitors dug-out with manager, Alan Dicks. Dicks' decision had been crucial. Rook's undoubted influence would now be sorely missed.

Gerry Ingram finally equalises for North End with just seven minutes to go

Straight back on the attack, a cross from McMahon found the head of Ingram but Gibson saved the ball low down on the City goal line. Gow then conceded a free kick and once more Spavin's kick caused an almighty scramble in front of the City goal. The ball was hoofed clear, but Heppolette regained possession on the left, ran through to the by-line and cut a centre back for Ingram to finally equalise with a shot from

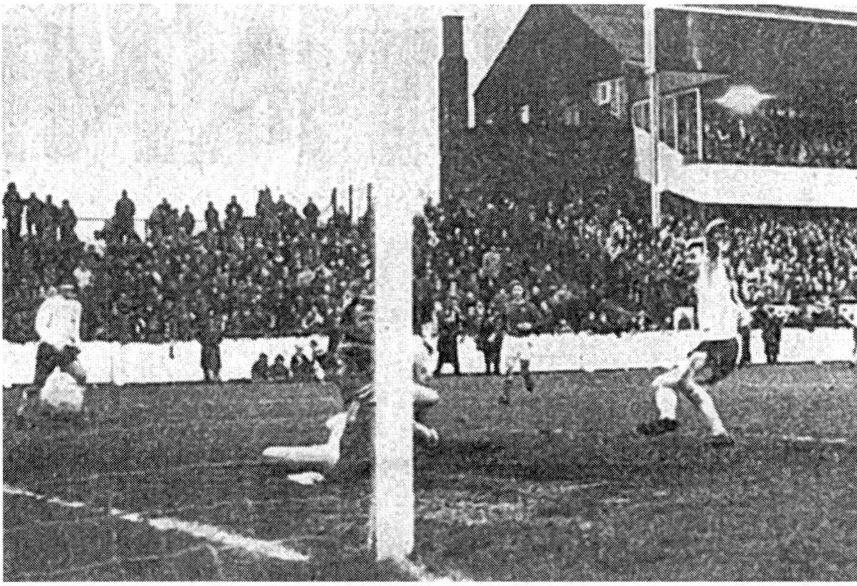

Top: Clive Clark gleefully puts North End ahead with six minutes to go
Bottom: ..and seals the amazing comeback taking the score to 4-2 in the 88th minute

close range with just seven minutes to go.

This suddenly had the Preston fans cheering with delight, and following the restart, they were cheering even louder as North End went 3-2 up with just six minutes left.

Merrick sliced a clearance out of the City box that went straight to Spavin who quickly brought it under control and pushed it forward to McIlmoyle, who quickly seized upon the open space in front of him.

Dashing to the right by-line, he hooked back a cross for the unmarked Clark to shoot gleefully home from six yards.

All of a sudden the crowd was in delirium after barracking not five minutes previously!

With two minutes remaining the shell shocked Robins conceded yet another goal that well and truly iced the North End cake. A North End move ended with Lyall's through ball being intercepted at pace by the sliding Clark who buried the ball into the back of the net, beating the advancing Gibson's dive.

What a comeback. What a game.

GRANDSTAND FINISH!

Spavin the key man in dramatic PNE win

North End had needed a lift after an extended New Year hangover which had seen defeats against Charlton Athletic and Luton Town, and the team tumble to mid table following the high of reaching fourth position just a month before.

More joy too on the following Monday, as North End were drawn at home to Manchester United in the next round, and hunt for a ticket was on!

There would be another development before the United tie however, one which would have significant repercussions and become a lasting financial millstone around North End's neck – the double signing of Neil Young and Dave Connor from Manchester City.

Neil Young (left)and Dave Connor sign for Preston North End watched by Alan Ball

CHAPTER 6

1971/72

PRESTON NORTH END V MANCHESTER UNITED
FA CUP 4TH ROUND, FEBRUARY 5TH 1972

'Preston North End will play.....Manchester United'

Despite an 'angry' denial in the press from Alan Ball just a few days before, North End announced the double signing of Dave Connor and Neil Young from Manchester City on January 20th 1972. Depending on your choice of newspaper, the reported fee ranged from £80,000 to £90,000 for the 'two-pack'.

The players were registered too late to appear in the next league game at Norwich, and Young was carrying an injury anyway. Connor made his debut at home the following week against Orient, while his ex-City colleague didn't appear in a Lilywhite shirt until February 12th.

The easiest way to get a ticket for the Manchester United game was to buy an official programme for the Orient home game the previous Saturday. There was a token printed on the inside back cover that assured you of a ticket as long as you were prepared to queue. Some 17,000 fans took advantage of this scheme, the rest of the tickets being sold down the usual routes to season ticket holders, fair-weather fans and of course the away contingent – United accounting for just under 10,000 tickets of various denominations.

North End were dealing with a raft of injuries to key players and there were major doubts hanging over Alex Spark, Ricky Heppolette, Graham Hawkins and the hero of the previous round, Clive Clark. As it transpired, it was only the latter pair who had to watch from the stands, with Alan Spavin taking over the captaincy from Hawkins.

The day dawned and I could think of nothing else. North End were featured on Grandstand's lunchtime 'Football Preview' programme which showed Alan Ball and the players earlier in the week during a coaching session at Deepdale. I set off a little earlier for the game and as usual caught the bus down to the junction of Ribbleton Lane and Skeffington Road.

Certainly a lot of fans must have had the same idea, and the walk down 'Skeffy Road' towards the ground was three abreast on the pavement with a solid wall of fans in front and behind. For some reason I stopped off at a newsagents just beyond the railway crossing on the corner of Castleton Road. I can't remember now what I went in for but I came out with a copy of the early edition of the LEP for that day as well, which doubled as a unique souvenir for the big match at Deepdale. That was carefully folded and placed with some degree of care into the large inside pocket of my 'parka'.

Rejoining the throng for the last leg of the journey to Deepdale, my last port of call was to queue for an official programme before making my way onto the Town End.

Well before the teams ran out, Deepdale was on the verge of bursting. The crowd is officially recorded as 37,052 and it was all of that. I could hardly move. All the usual fans I stood close to were nowhere to be seen – even Alf and John!

North End lined up:-

Kelly, McMahon, Connor, Bird, McNab, Spavin, Heppolette, Spark, McIlmoyle, Lyall, Ingram. Sub: Lamb

So here they were! Manchester United – standing fourth in Division One, just three points away from top spot, gracing the Deepdale pitch. It's worth noting their line up too:-

Stepney, O'Neil, Burns, Gowling, James, Sadler, Morgan, Kidd, Charlton, Law, Best. Sub: McIlroy

North End kicked off to a tremendous roar, their opening move ending when Hugh McIlmoyle couldn't prevent a through ball crossing the by-line for a United goal kick.

I was utterly mesmerised, and I make no apology for the fact that George Best was and still is my football hero. I watched him intently as the afternoon progressed. How he collected the ball, how he controlled and advanced with the ball – and on that particular day – how he was well restricted by new signing Dave Connor.

George Best tries to escape the attentions of John McMahon and Dave Connor

North End were playing it very tight at the back, and after a few minutes it was possible to see who the match ups were in front of Alan Kelly. Connor was marking Best, Jim McNab was taking on Denis Law, Spark was dealing with Bobby Charlton and John McMahon with Willie Morgan. United's early play surprisingly seemed to have striker Brian Kidd operating in a midfield role with Alan Gowling as the point of the visitor's attack. He was being watched by John Bird.

Alan Spavin got North End up field for the first time feeding a ball to Heppolette who appeared to be pushed over by full back Tommy O'Neill in the tussle for control. It didn't impress the referee though and as he waved play-on, was booed loudly.

Gerry Ingram challenges for the ball as Steve James heads clear for United

Back the ball came towards Kelly in the Kop goals. The North End defence, looking well on their toes and up for the battle, dealt with two corners won in quick succession by Best.

United were on top in these early stages and were trying to assert control. The ref was barracked again for not allowing Lyall to take a free kick quickly, but when Spavin finally floated the ball into the United box it caused the visitors all sorts of problems before being hacked clear by centre half Steve James.

United were suddenly appearing to be as tense as their hosts as they hesitated again, this time under a hanging Spavin corner. Once more the ball had to be hoofed unceremoniously clear, and it seemed that these 'superstars' may be fallible after all.

Kelly had to be at his very best as he sprinted to the edge of his box to deny Gowling, who had burst through a high and flat North End back line in pursuit of a Charlton through ball. A Lyall pass then sent Gerry Ingram galloping through in the inside right position, but the ball just had too much on it, and ran out of play.

Kelly was becoming busy, and drew gasps from the crowd when he just managed to grab a shot at the second attempt from Charlton with Law and Gowling in close attendance.

Alan Kelly (extreme right) collides with Alan Gowling after sprinting from his line

Law was in action again soon afterwards, leaping extraordinarily high to flick on a Best centre that beat the North End defenders, but not Kelly who managed to help the ball along its way with his fist.

United were applying some pressure now, and it was Kelly again to the rescue with a dive to keep out a low drive from Best. A Morgan free kick for a foul by Bird on Gowling looked dangerous as Best homed in on the ball, but Connor's boot was first there clearing the danger.

Ingram and McIlmoyle were North End's only outlet up front, but they were joined by Lyall in the 37th minute chasing down a lobbed pass forward from Spavin that Alex Stepney managed to get to first. Lyall then tried his luck with a fierce drive a couple of minutes later, but it flew high and wide into the Town End crowd.

Alan Kelly and Dennis Law receive treatment following a corner, while Dave Connor chats to his old Manchester adversary, George Best

The admirable McMahon was applauded loudly for dispossessing Morgan and calmly bringing the ball forward.

After interchanging passes with Lyall, he had progressed to a position from where he could have a decent shot at the United goal. The shot caused the home fans to cheer prematurely for a goal as the ball deflected off Spark and appeared to be running into the opposite corner of the net. Stepney had other ideas though, and incredibly twisted back to save near the goal line.

United were finding North End a tough nut to crack as half time neared. Ball's team could feel proud of themselves as they had tackled hard and were still in the game.

The half came to a close with Connor intercepting a pass intended for Best. The newcomer had impressed the home crowd so far and had limited the Irish star to just a few attempts on goal.

Taking in the Deepdale scene at half time, it was noticeable how the number of younger fans watching from the cinder track around the pitch had increased from just a few at kick off to what was now a forming circle of them now encompassing the hallowed turf – in places three and four deep. The police were busy trying to repatriate these fans with the terraces. From where I was standing, I was grateful that my mum had prepared a small flask of coffee along with some chocolate biscuits for me in my duffle bag. It would have taken me the rest of the match to navigate a way to the kiosk at the bottom corner of the terracing. Don't know how Alf would have coped!

I recall the half time chatter was mainly about North End's decent showing and, as one bloke near me chimed up, "...if they can just hold on there's always the chance they can score near the end." Not punditry of any great depth I agree, but I would certainly have settled for that scenario unfolding!

The groups of United fans mixed in with the Northenders on the Town End seemed a very over exuberant bunch – but then again who wouldn't be when you were watching their line-up every Saturday! They roared on every United pass – most unlike the reserved home supporters, who after years of struggle, were very careful when it came to handing out plaudits. They liked to see a move unfold first before getting too excited!

The North End players were given a big ovation as they trotted out for the second half. If we can't win, let's get a draw and take the cash at Old Trafford I thought as United started the second half. It was the visitors who probed forward first, but the attack broke down when Law was deemed to have handled the ball on the edge of the North End penalty area.

An under hit back pass to Kelly from McMahon brought cries of anguish from the home fans as Best, hovering behind the full back, almost intercepted the ball. Now in Kelly's face, he shadowed him closely as the keeper was trying to launch his drop kick, but the referee blew for a North End free kick, much to Best's muttering disdain.

Not one official, expert or pundit really quite knew why a successful attempt by Best in a similar situation with Gordon Banks during the Northern Ireland v England Home International in May 1971 had been disallowed. The clip is still available on You Tube for all to see. Nobody had ever done something like that before, and it certainly was, as David Coleman says on commentary, *"...a fascinating piece of football thinking by Best."*

It was North End's turn with the ball now and a cross from Heppolette with some potential brought both cheers and jeers as David Sadler was forced to hoof the ball on to the top of the West Stand in something of a hurry as Ingram and McIlmoyle were closing in.

Alex Spark hurriedly shoots wide and misses the chance to put North End ahead

North End spurned a chance to take the lead within a few minutes of the restart; the chance unfolding following a centre by the busy Lyall.

The ball was initially headed on by Spavin towards Ingram but just too far and quickly for the big forward to reach comfortably and control. He did however manage to poke the ball across and back to Spark, who taken a little by surprise, still managed to hastily hook a shot that veered wide of the angle of post and crossbar with Stepney rooted to the ground.

It was noticeable how Best had migrated from his position on the left to a more central midfield role, undoubtedly a feather in Connor's cap. Kidd was playing a little higher now, but the attack was still led by Gowling.

In the next United attack, Law trapped the ball on the by-line and directed it behind him into the path of Best whose low drive towards the near post brought a magnificent save from Kelly, the keeper at full stretch tipping the ball around the post for a corner.

United seem to be setting up camp at the Town End of the ground as they increased the pressure. Kelly made another excellent save , this time from Charlton, when he dived to his right to save a low drive, then got up and raced to collect the ball before it crossed the line for a corner.

A thoughtful and precise through ball by McIlmoyle for Lyall to run at came to naught as Lyall was too slow – or more than likely probably feeling the effects of a non-stop performance on a very heavy pitch.

Entering the last ten minutes, North End seemed spent and United went in for the kill. In a scintillating 10 second spell of play no fewer than three point bank United shots on goal were heroically blocked by the North End defence. It started with Best – reappearing on the left near the corner flag twisting and turning in front of Connor.

With McMahon lying prostrate in the six yard box, Best dispatches a great cross to the near post, where Heppolette leaps skywards for his life to tower above Morgan and head away. Spark heads the ball further away, but Best out jumps Connor and sends a towering header straight back into the danger area. Law, circling the edge of the box like a vulture, moves swiftly in and nods the bouncing ball forwards and down towards Morgan's feet. As he is teeing the ball up to shoot, Heppolette dives in with a superb blocking tackle, but the ball trickles back into the path of Law, now racing in to shoot. He meets the ball, but Bird with another magnificent block saves the day...only to see the ball squirt sideways and into the path of Charlton who has only Kelly between him and the North End net. Charlton calmly controls the ball and launches the inevitable missile from eight yards, but Kelly has moved forward quickly and smothers the ball which ricochets off his palms to the right...and safety.

Utter chaos in the North End goalmouth as Bobby Charlton launches the third United shot in 10 seconds at the North End goal – which was brilliantly saved by Alan Kelly

Time, which had flown by until now, was suddenly unfolding at a snail's pace as North End were put under the cosh. With just six minutes left, the dream was over.

O'Neill, moving out from the penalty area, made progress through the now deserted United half and passed infield to Best. He returned the ball to the full back now just 15 yards from North End's penalty area. The full back's curling centre was precisely aimed towards Law who leaped high above McNab to head forward and down directly into the path of Gowling whose run into the North End box had started as Law had begun his leap for the ball. The tall, makeshift striker-for- the-day took a touch as he shrugged off Bird's challenge and planted the ball firmly into the roof of the North End net from just five yards. The feeling in my stomach was sickening as the United fans jumped up and down and North End sloped back upfield for the kick off.

Top: Alan Gowling hits the ball high into the net for United's first goal
Bottom: Gowling scoops the ball into the net to complete his brace

Three minutes later the North End coffin lid was hammered shut as Gowling added a second goal as the home side threw all caution to the wind trying to land the equaliser.

Spavin, still utterly composed, curled a ball out to the right for Connor.

Immediately harried by Best, Connor turned towards his own goal looking for a way out and noticed Kelly was free. Still under pressure from the Irishman, Connor unfortunately sliced the ball out of play nearer to the corner flag than his keeper.

The difference in the two teams fitness levels was no better demonstrated than the moments that immediately followed. As United hared around getting into position quickly, North End sauntered back towards their penalty area. Indeed Best was able to strike the flag kick low and straight to the corner of the six yard box without a single white shirt in the vicinity. Charlton was able to amble towards the ball unhindered but delivered an air shot as the ball passed him by and carried on along the same line. Next to take aim at the coconut shy was Gowling who scooped the ball past Kelly and into the bottom corner despite Bird's best efforts.

And that was that. The North End team left the pitch to applause for their efforts but it was all tinged with such disappointment that even the 'glory' of a replay had been taken away from them in the closing minutes.

Ball blamed nobody for the defeat. When quizzed about Spark's miss, he replied *"He was playing his first game in six weeks and, like others, was feeling the strain. How could you be hard enough to blame the lad?"*

Forever positive, he continued, *"I was already working on my ideas for the replay when Alan Gowling snatched it away from us. But honestly, I can't say I was impressed with them. We were worth at least a goalless draw – and I'll tell you this. If we had gone to Old Trafford with Graham Hawkins back in the centre of defence and Neil Young in the attack, we would have been looking for more than just a percentage of the gate money."*

The long anticipated appearance on BBC's Match of the Day turned out to be a damp squib. For all the valiant endeavour North End had shown, the highlights were cut to the bone with just over five minutes actually

Front cover of the souvenir edition of the Lancashire Evening Post, February 5th 1972

transmitted, giving a very false impression of the match.

North End received a better ride with the press, and the next edition of the official programme listed selected comments from the LEP and the nationals.

Press Comments on Deepdale Cup-Tie

THE PRESS generally gave North End credit for a brave fight against Manchester United in last Saturday's F.A. Cup-tie, the majority view being that we at least earned a replay.

Lancashire Evening Post—North End can be proud of their effort....they stopped one of the best teams in Europe from scoring for 85 minutes. One sighed for absentees injured.

Sunday Mirror—Preston despite injuries gave every ounce of effort, and for a long time were slightly the better side. United looked a tired team of fading stars.

Sunday Times—Preston's solid defensive formation....gave United little scope for progress down the middle, but once they put on pressure there was only one team in it.

Sunday Telegraph—The difference between collective genius and sheer gameness finally cost Preston this Cup-tie. It seemed cruel that they should fall so late.

News of the World (Tommy Finney)—A flattering result that did not do full justice to Preston, whose defenders were heroes. To sum up United just had the edge.

People—The score does Preston an injustice. For 85 minutes they defied the aristocrats. More than that, they matched their opponents, and at times looked superior.

Sunday Express—The irony of it was that while Ball was planning for a replay Gowling was belatedly justifying his own manager's strategy....Preston did a man-size job.

Observer—United had been made to labour exhaustingly to achieve the insistent impetus that at last broke Preston's resistance. Both goals came in the last five minutes.

Sun—It was a game of cat-and-mouse before Preston ran out of steam and United were able to exert some control. Gowling collected a rich pay-off with two late goals.

Daily Express—United were tense and looked frightened of a team that fought valiantly only to see a replay chance stolen by the piracy of Alan Gowling.

Daily Mirror—United were contained and consistently challenged for a full 75 minutes by Preston....they failed partly because they were short of quality in the forwards.

Daily Telegraph—Preston never had the fire power to disturb Stepney. When their defence later was put under intense pressure United had established a moral ascendancy.

Daily Mail—Until they cast aside their caution and crashed through, United looked as if they, rather than injury-ravaged Preston were playing for a draw.

In 2015, when United were once again drawn to play at Deepdale in the FA Cup, John Bird was asked for his memories of the 1972 clash.

"It was a magnificent draw. And yes, you wondered how you would match up to them and that standard.

"But of course we were at home, Alan Ball senior was a great motivator and the atmosphere was unbelievable. There was a hell of a crowd.

"The line up would be more or less a 4-4-2, or a 4-3-3. I was playing centre-half with Alex Spark, John McMahon and Dave Connor were the full-backs, Jim McNab, George Lyall, Ricky Heppolette and Alan Spavin were the midfield. Spavin was the main man, the playmaker."

With the match still goalless inside those final minutes, Bird began to dream of a replay.

"I can remember thinking: Well, we've done well here, we haven't beaten them but the reward of going to Old Trafford was going to be unbelievable.

"And it was taken away from us. That's why we were disappointed because we knew we were in the game and we'd equalled them but lost."

After this particularly gallant effort, North End continued their slide down the Division Two table for the remainder of the 1971/72 season. The dizzy heights of the performance against Millwall were now a distant memory as Preston had to wait until March 11th to register their first league win since December 27th. Worst than that, they mustered just 10 points in total from their last 19 league outings finishing a dismal 18th.

The stress of managing North End took its toll on Ball, who suffered a mild heart attack towards the end of the season, whilst playing in a Sunday afternoon charity game at Nelson. It immediately followed a 1-4 home drubbing by Blackpool at Deepdale – and by his own admission Ball had been 'living on his nerves' in the weeks before that, desperately trying to guide his team to Division Two safety. His assistant, Arthur Cox took over while Ball recuperated for the last few games that finally saw North End survive the cut.

I asked Graham Hawkins a few years ago about this period; if there were off-field issues and if Ball had lost the dressing room.

He told me, *"Well, at any football club there is gossip and things going on off-field. As far as losing the dressing room or us not putting a shift in was concerned – absolutely not. Those seasons (1971/72, 1972/73) are remarkably similar. If there was a player/manager issue we wouldn't have got to fifth again during the following season. Bally got sacked the second time but there was no rejoicing in the dressing room – far from it."*

The height that Denis Law could generate from a leap for a header was mind-boggling. Here he is seen heading narrowly wide of the North End goal, early in the second half of the FA Cup tie at Deepdale.

CHAPTER 7

1972/73

FULHAM V PRESTON NORTH END
SEPTEMBER 2ND 1972

The assault on the summit begins

The new season hadn't really started for North End as we all kissed goodbye to August in 1972. Three league defeats, and one draw saw the Lilywhites bolted to the bottom of Division Two with just a single point and a solitary goal to their name – not forgetting the added discomfort of being dumped out of the League Cup by 'mighty' Workington Town.

As always, there were complications. Alan Lamb had broken his leg in the League Cup tie at Workington, and it was later discovered that Hugh McIlmoyle had broken a bone in his right foot during the same game. To compensate for the month's absence it would take McIlmoyle to recover, Alan Ball had managed to persuade Derby County manager, Brian Clough, to loan him his reserve centre forward Roger Davis.

It seemed like a good idea after his promising debut at Deepdale resulting in a draw with Queens Park Rangers, but following the midweek away defeat at Turf Moor, Clough told Ball he wanted Davis back immediately as he had his own injury crisis developing at the Baseball Ground.

The Turf Moor experience had further deepened Preston's woes, with the news that winger Clive Clark was now out of action with an ankle ligament injury. With little time left to do any more begging and borrowing, Ball had to look at what he had in his own back yard for the impending game against Fulham at Craven Cottage.

In the event, he added Alan Tarbuck and youngsters Alex Bruce and Mel Holden to the squad that left on the Friday afternoon Inter City train from Preston Station. Having slept on it, Ball decided to go with Tarbuck as the replacement for Davis and promote Bruce to substitute. North End lined up:-

Kelly, McMahon, McNab, Bird, Hawkins, Spavin, Wilson, Spark, Tarbuck, Young, Heppolette. Sub: Bruce

Fulham had only played three league matches so far, had a result of each denomination, which placed 18th in the table. Looking for some inspiration, North End wore red shirts and white shorts for this 'colour clash' outing – the same kit as they wore at Craven Cottage on May 1st 1971 when they pulled of a magnificent 1-0 win to achieve promotion from Division Three.

It was becoming essential that Preston broke their winless streak and moved off the foot of the table, but it was Fulham who dominated the early exchanges, and it was left to John McMahon to impress by showing a degree of coolness as he twice cleared North End's lines.

Fulham skipper Barry Lloyd unsurprisingly came off worst in a 50/50 tackle with Graham Hawkins and after a lengthy delay had to be stretchered off. He continued to receive treatment off the pitch near the home dug out, and after six minutes returned to the field of play to loud home cheers in a seemingly healthier state.

Now back to their full compliment, Fulham resumed their onslaught.

A Les Barrett corner causes consternation in the North End defence

Lloyd himself was only just off target with a diving header from a centre by Les Barrett on the right. Roger Cross then tried to lob Alan Kelly from 30 yards out, after the keeper had pushed away a corner but this attempt went high into the crowd.

North End had shown little or no attacking threat in the opening 20 minutes, barring a speculative Neil Young shot that went well wide. However, this was to change two minutes later when Young fired North End into a surprise lead.

Stan Brown, the Fulham half back, carelessly lost possession to Young just outside the home penalty area. With just one touch to steady himself, Young launched a fierce and rising drive across the box with his left foot that passed snugly between Peter Mellor's outstretched palm and the angle of post and crossbar as it found the net.

Much joy on the North End bench – and no less on the pitch as the players' clenched fists were clearly to be seen along with audible cries of encouragement to each other.

The goal certainly inspired North End, and they won a corner on the right after good work by McMahon and David Wilson. This led to an Alan Spavin centre from which Alex Spark put in a powerful header that flew just wide.

Fulham retaliated and Barrett should have done far better than slicing his shot well wide of Kelly's left post after a through ball from Brown. The left winger was at it again shortly afterwards, collecting a pass from defender John Richardson, but Jim McNab glided across the box to perform a perfectly judged tackle before Barrett could shoot.

When Young was crowded out near the Fulham box, Wilson stopped dangerous progress towards the North End box by conceding a foul on Lloyd. The resulting free kick caused some turmoil in the North End goalmouth before the reliable Graham Hawkins took control and headed the ball out for a corner. McMahon then gave away a second following Barrett's initial flag kick; this one causing all sorts of problems in front of the North End goal before John Bird punted the ball some distance to safety.

Back came the ball, and a menacing cross was headed backwards towards the North End goal by Richardson forcing Kelly to leap high and palm the effort over the bar with a magnificent save.

North End finally got mobile again, and Wilson had a right footed drive from 20 yards well saved by Mellor. The ball was punted downfield by Fulham as half time neared, and a well placed curling drive from home striker Steve Earle was just wide of Kelly's far post.

Another cross was launched into the North End box by left back Fred Callaghan and just as Hawkins rose above the rest to head away, the whistle sounded for half time.

The second half started well for North End. Young almost broke through the home defence on two occasions before finally winning a free kick 25 yards out. Another left foot thunderbolt was launched, passing the Fulham defenders along the way only to be about a foot too high to count.

A couple of Fulham raids were then made on the North End goal, both eventually broke down – the first stylishly intercepted by McMahon, playing with some degree of élan, and the second being blazed over the bar. It was from this goal kick that North End doubled their lead.

The clock had ticked to the 57th minute when Alan Tarbuck collected Kelly's downfield punt and sped off down the left flank. Tarbuck's low centre met Wilson running into the box from the right at the near post. He made no mistake in flicking the ball into the net for his first goal for North End for quite some time.

Suddenly, the Fulham fans became disheartened with their team. They started howling at them constantly, and all this was helping the Preston cause. Tarbuck was buzzing around everywhere and was hauled down at the expense of a free kick. McMahon centred, but this was pushed away by Mellor but only to Young whose volley went over the bar.

The irrepressible Tarbuck was at it yet again – picking up the ball, carrying it forward at speed and tormenting centre half Paul Went before passing to Ricky Heppolette on the left wing. 'Heppy' crossed the ball quickly having seen Wilson move in again across the box from the right. The winger met the ball perfectly on the volley and the ball rocketed into the back of the net leaving Mellor looking as though he had been glued to the ground.

Alan Tarbuck wriggles his way through the Fulham defence yet again

What a strike, and very well deserved too. Wilson had given his marker Callaghan the complete and utter run around thus far and he deserved the team's congratulations that were being heaped upon him.

Fulham were in 'heads down' mode now as North End steadied the game right down and totally dominated proceedings. Fulham manager Alec Stock brought on John Cutbush for the now limping Cross but it made little difference.

Young collected a through ball from Spavin on the left, progressed forward and watched his low shot fly past Mellor, hit the far post and bounce to safety. After two more close calls, Ball substituted Young and gave Alex Bruce a run-out. This appeared to be no reflection on Young's play, (he received an ovation from the home crowd), with the North End manager giving him a pat on the back as he walked off.

Fulham launched a late desperate surge and pulled a goal back, when Richardson pushed up into permanent attack, ran on to a Barrett pass and shot past Kelly into the corner of the net.

North End had a penalty appeal turned down almost immediately afterwards when Heppolette appeared to be upended but the referee waved play on. The final whistle was greeted with near silence by the home fans who had seen their team thoroughly outmanoeuvred.

It was an excellent North End performance, from back to front. The defence stood firm and were rarely troubled. The midfield was mastered by the trio of Spavin, Spark and Heppolette and the attack never allowed the Fulham defenders to relax.

GOLDEN PRESTON

PRESTON North End manager Alan Ball got his "show on the road" **at last today** when his team gained their first win of the season by **beating Fulham** 3-1 at Craven Cottage.

The star turn was Dave Wilson, who scored two goals as Preston turned on the heat in the second half.

His first came from a centre by Alan Tarbuck and his second from a cro... Ricky He...

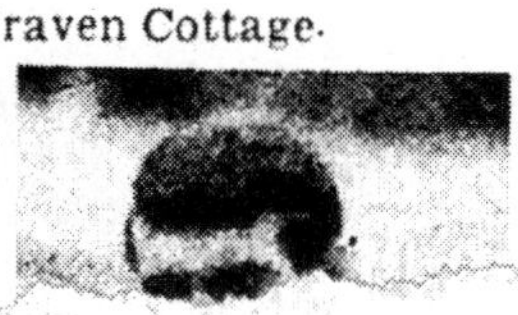

led to disaster just before the interval but, the attack fizzled out.

Hawkins then outjumped his opponents to head away a dangerous free ...

When asked why had he taken off the dangerous Young with 14 minutes still on the clock, Ball replied, *"I thought his ankle had gone again – but it's ok, and I was being nagged by young Bruce, who wanted a run."*

This was the start of an excellent run of form for North End, lasting well into December which saw them steadily climb to the heights of the Division. However, nobody could possibly have foreseen the turmoil and woe that would descend over the club before the season was over...

CHAPTER 8

1972/73

PRESTON NORTH END V BRIGHTON & HOVE ALBION NOVEMBER 25TH 1972

Another win…another great run…then the wheels come off – again!

The away win at Fulham on the first Saturday of September 1972 had a quite amazing effect on North End. With a further six league games to contest during the month, four were won and two were drawn. This glorious run had taken them from bottom spot on the first day of the month, to fourth on the last day.

The run continued; wins and draws were more regular then defeats – of which there were just three to register between September 1st and the Brighton & Hove Albion contest, due to take place at Deepdale on November 25th.

North End were back in a good place again. They were performing well above expectations and Ball had proved to both the board and the fans that he could recover a grave situation. The football style was good. At home Preston would attack down the flanks and play an entertaining style, and in David Wilson and Clive Clark – although both were a little long in the tooth – Ball had as good a wing pair as any outside Division One. On their travels, North End would break quickly, and invariably pinch a goal knowing that they could rely on statistically the best defence in the section, expertly marshalled by Graham Hawkins and his deputy John Bird, to resist anything and everything the home team could throw at them.

The manager's startling reflection whilst convalescing at the end of the previous season that North End had 'made a mistake' in purchasing Neil Young seemed to have been largely forgotten and he was now a regular in the team. There was no way North End could ever recoup or improve on their outlay for the former Manchester City midfield stroller, so it looked as though Alan Ball had wiped the slate clean and had just got on with utilising the stock he had.

Being a young and ever hopeful wide eyed fan, it was puzzling and somewhat distressing to regularly read that first teamers who were performing well were being openly offered to rivals. Granted, *'transfer windows'* didn't exist back then – a club was free to buy or sell until the transfer deadline day in late March – but surely, was this really the way forward?

On the eve of this very game, with North End tucked in just behind the league leaders, LEP readers were regaled with the news that Hugh McIlmoyle and Ricky Heppolette were in talks with Carlisle United and Orient respectively, with a view to being moved on as soon as possible. A similarly ridiculous state of affairs had occurred at the end of the previous season when the extremely popular and useful George Lyall was repeatedly offered to various rivals, before eventually being snapped up by Nottingham Forest, while Ball was convalescing after his heart attack.

The boardroom games carried on however. Ball was obviously operating under a 'sell-and-see-if-we-will-let-you-buy' diktat which was quite illogical, considering the high league position his management had taken North End. Surely he needed backing?

It was no real wonder that the fans – despite North End's lofty position – were apathetic about the club and were voting with their feet. Just 8,005 turned up for the contest with Brighton who arrived at Deepdale occupying 21st place in Division Two, with only Cardiff City below them. Even with their team a racing certainty to win, the paying spectators were wearying of the board's methods.

It was a typical late November day in industrial Lancashire – slate grey skies, occasional rain…and cold. Perhaps the south coast boys didn't really fancy taking on in-form North End, but throwing the weather conditions in too must have surely added to their woes.

I remember this match quite well as one of my earlier North End childhood heroes, Willie Irvine, was in the Brighton team. I was looking forward to seeing him play at Deepdale again, two years or so after his departure.

North End lined up with :-

Kelly, McMahon, McNab, Bird, Hawkins, Spavin, Wilson, Spark, McIlmoyle, Young, Bruce. Sub: Clark

North End were quick on the attack, and a cross from Neil Young saw a Graham Hawkins header go just over the Brighton crossbar.

The visitors' tactics seemed to be to crowd Alan Spavin out at every opportunity and stop him playing. It was a compliment in reality, but while the men in red and black stripes enveloped Spavin, they were leaving massive gaps all around the field.

Despite this attention, 'Spav' was still performing his magic, seemingly relishing performing on the soft and sodden surface. He broke free of this 'jailers' at one stage and curved a lovely ball into the box only to see the Brighton keeper, Alan Dovey, make a scrambling save.

After around 15 minutes, Brighton put together a decent move that was ended when Alan Kelly easily collected Bert Murray's centre. Amazingly this was the first time Kelly had touched the ball since the pre match warm-up. There had been little to see from Willie Irvine, bar the odd touch of the ball here and there, but he did lay off a nice pass to Eddie Spearrit, whose shot was saved by Kelly.

After more Preston pressure, Murray broke away, cut in from the right, and was bearing down on goal with North End caught on the hop. His shot went across the face of goal however, and Peter O'Sullivan's follow up shot thankfully only found the side netting.

The play swung to the other end sharply, and a tackle on Dave Wilson in the Brighton box brought loud appeals for a penalty – the referee waving play on as the ball bounced out for a corner. Young swung the flag kick in perfectly and midfielder Alex Spark saw his header cleared off the line by Spearrit with Dovey well beaten.

It wasn't long before the inevitable happened, and North End duly took the lead via the boot of their brightest prospect for years, Alex Bruce.

Alex Bruce slams the ball home for North End's opener against Brighton

Spavin split the visitors defence wide open with a superb pass that Bruce made no mistake with; finishing the move without fear with a low drive that flew past the diving Dovey. It was a great goal and the North End team ran up to congratulate the young Scot.

As the first half neared its end, Irvine managed to get a header on target but it was competently dealt with by Kelly. Play then switched back to the other end, and by now North End were playing their best football of the match.

Right at the end of the half, North End were awarded a penalty to further compound Brighton's woes. Hugh McIlmoyle, progressing through the visitor's box, fell to the ground when tackled by Brighton stalwart Norman Gall – the spot kick being confirmed without hesitation by the referee. It was a decision that didn't go down well and as Brighton argued with the ref, Young placed the ball to his liking on the penalty spot.

The 'conflab' over, Young fired home the penalty firmly and wide of Dovey's dive into the back of the net.

The general opinion at half time was that it had been, "too easy" for North End. "It's a long way to come play rubbish like that," said John – and it was a fair point. Brighton, apart from two or three probing runs had been mainly concerned with halting Spavin and packing their box. It didn't bode well for their fans back home who, no doubt, were enjoying much better weather conditions than we were at that moment!

No sooner had the second half kicked off, than North End were three up! The visitors were caught upfield and Wilson, moving down the right at speed towards the Kop after leaving left back George Ley on the deck, crossed the ball into the Brighton box. It was absolutely the right thing to do, as the only people in the area were McIlmoyle and Jim McNab of Preston, the referee and the Brighton 'keeper, Dovey.

The ball swung in high over the six yard line and was contested by leaps from both McIlmoyle and Dovey, whilst McNab stayed grounded just a few yards behind. Although Dovey's hands touched the ball, it was never under his full control, and fell behind him as both he and

McIlmoyle came down to earth. With the ball rolling loose straight into the path of McNab, the North End left back took full advantage and scored probably the easiest goal in Deepdale's long history as he simply stroked the ball home from five yards into the empty net.

Brighton protested that Dovey had been pushed, but to no avail. The referee had been quite close to the incident and would have none of it.

Five minutes later, Brighton put their best move of the match together, when after neat play, O'Sullivan found ex- Chelsea striker Barry Bridges in the penalty area with a pass from the right. Bridges was never really in control of the ball, but still managed to somehow bounce it past the advancing Kelly and towards the North End goal line. With all eyes on the Town End focused on the ball heading for the unguarded net, it was a great relief to see 'Mr Reliable' – Hawkins – fly through everybody's right sided peripheral vision and slide the ball away for a corner. Cue John's usual "G'lad Lerch! Best signing we ever made that lad....." as the rest of us applauded our captain's latest heroic deed.

North End's confidence soon returned and another good move involving Young and Spavin ended with Bruce firing just wide. The ever enthusiastic John McMahon then raced down the right and sent in a cross that came back off the Brighton crossbar before being pushed out for a corner. An infringement against North End from the flag kick enabled the visitors to wriggle off the hook.

The limping O'Sullivan was replaced by striker Ken Beamish as Brighton sought some form of consolation from the game.

The game sprang into life suddenly when Spark carefully aimed a through ball for Young to run on to, but his rocket shot was deflected for yet another corner by Dovey. It was curled in to perfection by Young as Hawkins rose above the 'keeper and headed downwards towards the bottom right corner from around the penalty spot. Screams of anticipation from behind the Kop goal turned to anguish as Spearitt somehow kept his mind clear enough to assess the situation in an instant and hook the ball well clear.

It wasn't long before North End struck again. Bruce broke through the Brighton back line, ran forward, drew Dovey and slotted the ball into the back of the net. Such maturity from 19 year old Bruce, who was undoubtedly a star rapidly ascending.

There was still time for Spark to drive in a good shot as North End continued their search for a fifth goal, but it was tipped over the bar. As the corner was taken, the referee blew the final whistle and North End trotted into the dressing room to well earned, resounding ovation.

THAT'S MORE LIKE IT!

PNE pictures by Bud [illegible]

..but Ball almost missed PNE win

By NORMAN SHAKESHAFT

MANAGER Alan Ball almost missed Preston's biggest win of the season against bottom of the Second Division Brighton at Deepdale on Saturday.

He had meant to go to Leyton to see the Orient forwards in action against Sheffield Wednesday with a view to taking one of them in a part exchange deal for North End midfield man Ricky Heppolette. But, when Ball got as far as the station at Manchester he suddenly changed his mind and returned to Preston.

He was delighted with the decision, for North End ended their goal famine at last by scoring four times without reply.

They had managed only five goals in eight previous home games, but, this time, they never looked like losing.

Alex Bruce opened the scoring with a good shot from an Alan Spavin pass, Neil Young converted a penalty for a foul by Norman Gall on Hugh McIlmoyle, Jim McNab netted from close range, after Brighton goalkeeper Alan Dovey had dropped the ball when challenged by McIlmoyle, and Bruce set the seal on the win when he broke through, ran forward, drew Dovey and slotted the ball home.

Bruce has now scored four times in Preston's last four matches, and is beginning to fulfil the promise he has shown for so long.

North End's victory was based on their strength in [illegible]

• Alex Bruce (third from right) scores North End's first goal with a low shot.

• *Prelude to a goal as Hugh McIlmoyle challenges Brighton 'keeper Alan Dovey (left), with Jim McNab close at hand . . . the ball went loose and (right) McNab scores Preston's third.*

Once again they hadn't conceded a goal, but had heavily improved the 'goals for' column. They proudly stood fourth and fully deserved their lofty perch near the top of the division.

From this point however, matters both on and off the pitch – just as in the season before – took a nosedive.

On the pitch, North End followed the Brighton win with a hard fought draw against Huddersfield Town at Leeds Road, gaining praiseworthy acknowledgement from Ian Greaves, the 'Terriers' manager in the process. *"This is the best Preston side I can remember. They have experience, blend and a tremendous team spirit."* The downside of that day was the involvement of Alan Ball in an unsavoury incident which resulted in him being reported to the authorities by the referee. It concerned an injured Jim McNab, and whether he should have been on or off the field of play to receive treatment.

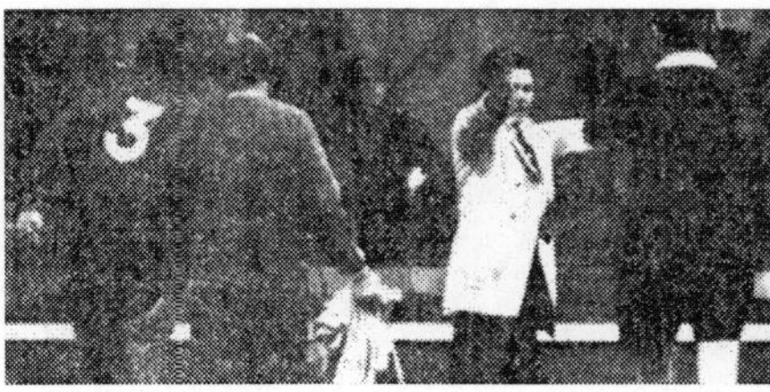

Left: Jim McNab (No.3) clutches his thigh while Alan Ball assails referee Ralph Lee
Right: Ball sticks to his guns and Mr Lee takes restraining action

The local derby against free-scoring Blackpool (third in Division Two) was up next at Deepdale. There was a massive build up to this game, and it was billed as the clash of *'the irresistible force against the immovable object.'* Sadly for North End the 'irresistible force' proved too strong for them and they lost 0-3, a score line which flattered the Seasiders somewhat; North End conceding two late goals after throwing everyone forward in desperate search of an equaliser.

Back with their bit between their teeth, North End gleaned another valuable away point with a goalless draw at Roker Park, with both sides missing a penalty. Managers Ball and Bob Stokoe were often arguing on the touchline and both had to be spoken to by the referee.

The pre-Christmas game at home to Bristol City produced a 3-3 thriller but was watched by just 7,700 fans, no doubt many of them sickened by the news that Heppolette's non-participation was due to the fact he was in London about to sign for Orient.

And so to Boxing Day. The first wheel well and truly fell off with a 6-1 pummeling at the hands of Carlisle United at Brunton Park. The players were called in on their subsequent days off by Ball following this annihilation and it seemed to pay off as Luton Town were beaten 2-0 at Deepdale just before the New Year, (Ball was accused by Luton Town in the days following of using underhand tactics against them during this match).

The turn of the year was heralded by one shocking performance after another; a 0-3 defeat at Queens Park Rangers, removed easily from the FA Cup by Grimsby Town after a dreadful display in a replay at Deepdale, (Ball in a fist fight with a Grimsby supporter at the end of the match at Blundell Park), a comprehensive 0-3 defeat at home to Fulham, a 6-2 hammering by Hull City at Bootherferry Park and what was to be Ball's last stand as manager – a 0-5 mauling at the hands of Portsmouth in front of a paltry 6,230 fans at Deepdale on February 10th.

Ball's sacking certainly caused much debate. There had been fans at Deepdale who had watched every home game who shouted, 'Ball Out, Ball Out' towards the end of his tenure. They wouldn't be placated; this was all down to Ball and he should go.

At 16 years of age, I just couldn't believe that this had happened roughly at the same time for two seasons running. I didn't shout for Ball's head. I was much more interested in what was going on behind the scenes; the root cause of it, if you will. Why would Ball say to the directors *"Gentelmen – which of you is resigning?"* upon being sacked?

I couldn't get my head around it all back then. But now, I think I can!

CHAPTER 9

BALL, THE BOARD AND THE AFTERMATH

The fallout following the dismal North End display against Portsmouth at Deepdale was to be both tumultuous and enduring. The starting gun was fired the following day. After a specially convened 3pm Sunday board meeting it was agreed unanimously to prepare the following statement and release it on Monday morning after the formal dismissal of Alan Ball.

"After discussion it was unanimously resolved by the board that Mr. Alan Ball's position as manager of the club be terminated forthwith. Arrangements are in hand for the appointment of a caretaker manager. The position of team manager will be advertised."

As recently as six months previously a couple of board members had stood behind Ball, smiling as he signed a new three year contract. It was around the time he had won the Division Two 'Manager of the Month Award' for September, in a period when North End were producing some fine football week in, week out. He had also been the bookmakers second favourite to take over at Manchester United in mid-December following Frank O'Farrell's dismissal. Now he was left holding his notice, while handing over the keys to his car.

Recently appointed assistant manager Frank Lord would now take over the reigns until the end of the season.

North End find a scapegoat

PRESTON North End's board of directors has made Alan Ball the scapegoat for the club's failures in the past two months. Now, immediately, the conjecture must begin as to who will take over as team manager at Deepdale.

Mr Tom Nicholson, the Preston chairman, has appointed Frank Lord caretaker manager and he will get on with the job pending the appointment of a new man after the post has been advertised.

But former Manchester United boss Frank O'Farrell is the clear favourite for a permanent position.

He has been out of a job since United sacked him in December, but has always been liked and respected at Deepdale, where he played as one of the stars of the North End First Division team of the late 50's.

The problem is that his finances have not been sorted out yet, since he left Old Trafford, although United are said to be prepared to honour the remaining part of what was a £12,000 a year five-year contract.

Ironically, Ball was one of the men linked with the United job after O'Farrell was sacked and before Tommy Docherty, another former Preston player, was appointed.

Comment By NORMAN SHAKESHAFT

Ball was thought to have the fiery qualities which O'Farrell lacked and which were needed by the First Division club.

Ball has had a rough deal at Deepdale, but the players seem to have turned against him in the end, and he has never been given the right kind of support from the board.

It seems to me that Ball has paid the penalty for a major blunder in draining the club's finances in the £80,000 deal for Neil Young and Dave Connor just over a year ago.

I hope that the board can find more money at last for a new man so that he can have the opportunity of rectifying things, but they will first have to pay a hefty sum out to Ball and this will be another crippling blow.

He still has nearly two - and - a - half years of a £7,000 a year contract to run and has told the board that he has put the matter in the hands of his solicitors. If he is paid out fully he will have been given adequate compensation although he is a bitterly disappointed man.

Meanwhile, the danger signals are bright red for North End.

Ball was confident that he could have done the job for which he has been paid but now Preston will have to find someone who they think can succeed where he is alleged to have failed.

This will not be easy and I doubt if any manager could have won the Third Division championship in his first year and kept the team so high in the Second Division up to December.

Ball has made many enemies of course. His outbursts and his attitude have got him into trouble several times and three recent incidents have upset a lot of people.

The first came when he clashed with a referee at Huddersfield on December 2nd, the second followed when he was reported for making comments after the victory over Luton on December 30th and the last was when he was involved in a punch up with a spectator after the cup-tie at Grimsby last month.

It may well be that the Football League or the Football Association may

Turn to Back

BALL SACKED

ALAN BALL was today sacked as Preston North End manager after just two and a half years at Deepdale. He learned the news from the directors, but was adament about his capabilities.

"I have never been a failure; I am not a failure now and I am not leaving Preston as a failure," he said. "This morning I turned to the men who have sacked me and said: 'Gentlemen which of you is resigning?'"

He added that none of them replied. But in an official statement, the chairman, Mr Tom Nicholson, said the decision to sack Ball had been unanimous.

The statement said: "At a meeting of the board it was unanimously resolved that the services of Mr Alan Ball as manager of the club be terminated forthwith. Arrangements are in hand for the appointment of a caretaker manager. The position of team manager will be advertised."

[illegible]

WHAT THE FANS THINK SEE PAGE SEVEN

Happier times at Preston

[illegible]

Lancashire Evening Post front page, 12th February 1973

The LEP devoted its front page to the story in all its Monday editions, and Norman Shakeshaft, their Preston North End correspondent at the time, voiced his opinion that Ball had been made a scapegoat, *"...simply the board have not been able to provide him with the money necessary to strengthen the team..."* whilst also observing that the board were equally only too willing to sell off Ball's best players.

This aspect of the Ball sacking has its roots in the Sixties, centring around the desire of North End's Peter Thompson, David Wilson (both England U23's), and Howard Kendall (England youth) to further their careers at a higher level. Huge bids for that era were made for the wingers both collectively and individually, but the board wanted to keep hold of them if at all possible. They eventually relented and sanctioned Thompson's move to Liverpool to hopefully take the heat out of the situation, but were determined to keep Wilson and his written transfer request was refused. He wasn't happy and eventually a League tribunal intervened on his behalf in October 1966. In the meantime, Kendall made a request for a transfer which was also refused.

A second request from Kendall was submitted, and Liverpool applied more pressure on the board, offering £75,000 for his services. It was noted at a board meeting that under the regulations at that time, Kendall would have to be offered a new contract when he turned 21 years of age – just a year away. At that point he could refuse it and freely demand to be transferred. It was agreed by the directors that Kendall would therefore have to be sold, but to quell any bad public feeling towards the board, a different statement was put out to the AGM, stating simply that Kendall's request had been refused.

In February 1967, Wilson's transfer fee was set by the tribunal at a ridiculously low £20,000, and he was quickly recruited to the Liverpool ranks. In the event, this particular saga had cost the North End Board tens of thousands of pounds – a mistake they ensured would never happen again; in future they would 'cash-out' early.

Soon afterwards, Kendall met the chairman and was adamant that he wanted first division football. Within a short period of time his transfer to Everton was confirmed, to avoid any possible reduction in the board's £80,000 valuation (equating to £1.4M in 2018).

The PNE Board meeting minutes of February 26th 1967 are significant, recording the following stated aims and future direction of the board after effectively having their fingers burned over the transfers of Wilson and Kendall. ***"It was generally agreed that the acquisition of higher priced players would present too many problems for a club of our standing."***

As a consequence, for the next 27 years those emerging talents moved on early would be replaced by players 'who had been around the block.' The North End spiral of decline had been set in motion.

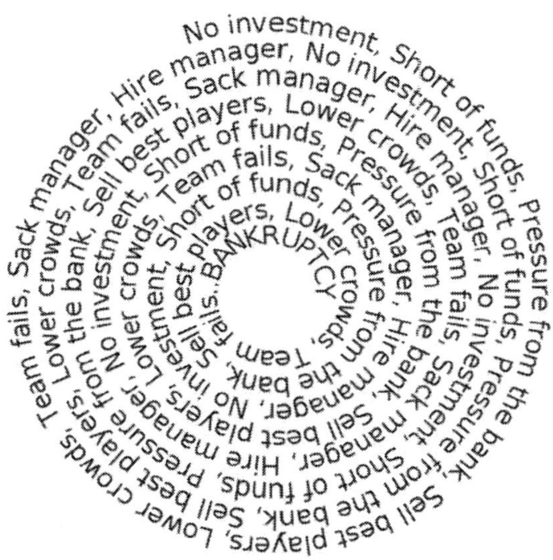

The 'Football Spiral of Decline' – a chart used to demonstrate how a football club with low ambition suffers consequential decline

It was the Baxi Partnership purchase of North End in September 1994 that finally arrested the hopeless decline and transformed the club. It was music to the long suffering fan's ears that millions of pounds would be spent, *"...on a stadium that everyone would like to have...and there has got to be investment on the playing side too, and it is our role to make funds available,"* said incoming chairman, Bryan Gray. Backed by his vision, North End would be transformed from a team wallowing in the league basement into a correctly guided and proud club competing in the play-off final for a Premiership place within just seven years.

Of course, North End weren't the only 'town club' faced with these aforementioned dilemmas of in the early Seventies, indeed all the surrounding Lancashire clubs suffered at one point or another. The singularly major problem that North End had was that they didn't own their own ground, Deepdale.

Back in March 1971, the club assets were valued at approximately £85,000 – consisting of the Willow Farm training capacity, club houses, and the Pavilion Stand. The club could not raise a decent overdraft at any of the banks with such low financial security and were in effect beholden to them. When costs mounted, the overdraft grew and as regularly as clockwork another player of promise or note had to be hawked for immediate sale. The overdraft then became under control until the costs eventually reached the limit again and the cycle would repeat '*ad nauseum*' becoming an ever narrowing spiral.

The fact that Ball had reached such a lofty position in Division Two in December 1971, replicated exactly a year later, whilst working within these confines, affords him immense credit. The pressure of delivering a successful team must have been enormous knowing that at any moment the bank, through the board, could initiate the sale of yet another member of his first team.

It is often reasoned when a football club's directors are under fire, *"well, how would you like all that abuse and disrespect if you were putting your own money into the club?"* This may well be pertinent in many cases, but quite astoundingly was not true of the North End Board. Records show that the generally established procedure of directors submitting personal cash guarantees to cover the bank overdraft seemed to have ceased in the mid 1930's! A director's only investment risk was confined to their personal shareholding in the company, and these were far from huge stakes.

As a consequence, the board was seemingly doing nothing more than gathering regularly to execute the demands of the bank.

Whether it was Alan Ball, Bobby Charlton or even Sir Alf Ramsey, these were the facts of life for the incumbent manager at Deepdale. His success would depend upon his skill in the transfer market – identifying likely prospects and selling them on for a profit.

What a pity then, that after identifying the player of the decade at the chrysalis stage, the board failed to support Ball's judgement over Scunthorpe's Kevin Keegan. Dithering over just a few thousand pounds, they allowed Liverpool to barge past and lift the golden fleece. Of course, the board didn't have to answer to anyone for their stunning self-inflicted fail!

A negative often levelled at Ball was the burdening purchase of Neil Young and David Connor from Manchester City. I beg to differ. Ball did not approve any player purchases – and certainly not hire purchase agreements – that was the board's remit. Any manager under the pressure that Ball was experiencing would obviously have grabbed any board proposal of new players with both hands.

The facts are that Ball didn't in fact chase these players down, they appear to have been a package offered to North End by Manchester City, at a time when the financially lucrative Manchester United cup tie was looming on the horizon. The board obviously thought that City's proposal of a £10,000 down payment followed by 35 payments of £2000 a month, incurring an additional total interest charge of £8890 was therefore within their compass. It was folly. The club finances were so poorly managed that by August 1972, North End had regularly defaulted on their repayments and the debt to City had already risen to £121,000. The pressure of this ineptitude would eventually fall upon the managers' shoulders as he would be stripped of yet another first team asset.

Relieving a post heart attack, convalescing and absent Ball of the services of George Lyall, sold to Nottingham Forest for around £40,000 earlier in May 1972, PNE Chairman Tom Nicholson said, *"…we were well over the figure that we are allowed to be overdrawn at the bank and the fee will improve our finances and enable us to pay the clubs wages during the summer, when we have no cash coming in through the turnstiles."* So, funds for continued existence were absolutely necessary from player sales and the fans, but there was still no hint of any boardroom contributions or possible inventive solutions to break free of the financial dilemma the club was floundering in! It had seemingly become just too easy to sit back and carry on as before.

It was this supine attitude that was the real problem.

One can only imagine the pressure and subsequent frustrations Ball was repeatedly coming up against, but his randomly outspoken manner certainly wasn't helping matters. Towards the end of his tenure at Deepdale his behaviour was becoming increasingly erratic with polarising media-hyped incidents at Huddersfield and Grimsby, where on both occasions he clashed with the home fans. The Luton Town allegation from the end of December was also still outstanding on the charge sheet. Asked if these incidents had been an element in the sacking, Nicholson replied, *"partly."*

Shakeshaft intimates in his article that Ball had lost the confidence of his team. On page 66, I have already related captain Graham Hawkins' view that this just wasn't the case. It's not as though the team picked up immediately following Ball's departure either, which would have lent some credence to the allegation.

Hawkins recalled that Frank Lord's caretaker management style was amongst the most peculiar he had ever witnessed. *"There certainly wasn't the depth of thought on the tactical side as there was with Bally, and he had players playing out of their usual positions which wasn't needed and very confusing. 'Spav' was also sidelined which didn't go down well at all."*

Lord's brief was to guide the good ship North End to safer waters and avoid relegation, but unfortunately for him it was to be played out against a lingering and distracting backdrop of player discontent, crowd demonstrations and proposed board takeovers.

The first outing was to Villa Park, where a plucky 1-1 draw was gained, but then North End went down to Sheffield Wednesday at Hillsborough; taking the lead with an Alan Tarbuck goal but eventually succumbing to a late Wednesday winner and losing by 2-1.

The crowd demonstrations were organised sensibly, and were orderly. The protesters called themselves the 'Deepdale Action Group' and gathered regularly for meetings at local hostelries around the town. They would not boycott the games as they realised that in the current scheme of things, attendance takings were vital to North End.

Soccer fans organise protest over Ball sacking

A PETITION condemning the Preston North End board of directors over the sacking of former manager Alan Ball was organised today when sandwich board men went through the town centre collecting signatures.

A total of 8,000 leaflets have been printed and the wording is "We the undersigned wish to register our disapproval of the recent conduct of the directors of Preston North End FC in their summary dismissal of the manager, Alan Ball.

"We further wish to demonstrate our feeling that this dismissal reflects upon the lack of responsibility shown by the directors to the public and, that by this action, Ball has been made a scapegoat for the directors."

The organisers are Mr Chris Duxbury of Plungington-road, Preston, and Mr Ken Phillips of Chaddock-street, Preston, who both work in the treasurer's department at the county hall, and who are keenly interested in football.

"We hope that all 8,000 leaflets will be signed and that we will then be able to present them to the board," said Mr Duxbury, who is seen collecting a signature in Fishergate.

The 'Deepdale Action Group' garnering support on the streets of Preston

They saw the directors as the root cause for the crisis, and even turned up outside the Millwall ground in the middle of March to vent their grievances to the them as they arrived on the team coach. They had collected around 5,000 signatures outside Deepdale before the home draw against Swindon Town – the total attendance was 6,468 – so it could actually be argued they largely represented the views of the paying fan. The response to this was for the directors to rather ill-advisedly label the group *'clueless'* which merely fanned the flames further.

Despite the fact there was no improvement in the trend of results after Lord's first two games in charge, (he was making similar noises to those Ball had, *"I want a forward who can nick 'em in"*), the board continued just as before and sold centre forward Tarbuck to Shrewsbury Town for a reported £16,000. Lord soon found out there was nobody making the incoming journey, and his task had just got that bit harder.

DEEPDALE ACTION GROUP

REQUESTS THE PLEASURE OF YOUR COMPANY AT THE HOME GAME WITH **CARDIFF CITY** on **SAT. MARCH 24th**

It's the players we love, the directors we hate,
So give the lads an increase in gate.

MAKE THIS THE FIRST WIN OF 1973

DAG flyers urged fans to continue to turn up and support the team

Lord's struggle continued, and a heavy 4-1 defeat at Millwall was followed by a another at the hands of Sunderland and a goalless draw against Cardiff City, both at Deepdale. On the following Monday morning March 26th, the Daily Mirror broke a story headlined, **'Spavin blow for Preston.'**

It revealed that Alan Spavin wanted to leave Deepdale – and the sooner the better! *"After 15 years with Preston, he has asked for his contract to be cancelled and, if this request is turned down, Spavin will quit the game."* This was astounding – but by the time the LEP was published later that day, the board had already released Spavin from his contract, but kept his registration, thus preventing him from joining any other club without a transfer fee being paid to Preston first.

The crux of the matter seemed to revolve around events at team level since the sacking of Ball. Spavin said:

"I didn't mind being dropped, but I would have thought that I would have been asked to help with the reserves or work in some other capacity. This hasn't happened, and I haven't even been spoken to."It has caused me some heart searching to create this rift with the club, but it is time somebody said something about the situation at Deepdale before it's too late."

Shakeshaft revealed later in the article that, *"Spavin added that several other players feel the same way about matters but are not in a position to walk away. Certainly some of the most experienced men on North End's books have told me they are fed up with the way things have gone this season. They say that they disagreed with the dismissal of Ball, a man who they respected and who was a 'player's manager'."*

The ante was upped the following day in the LEP when Lord replied to Spavin's allegations in an article headed **'He rocked the boat says Lord.'**

"I have been trying to set the ship right and improve the side – that is my job. Spavin has no reason to say the things he has said – it is not my fault he has not been playing well. I have been a successful manager for four years in South Africa and I don't want to fail here. I am straight with everyone, and I expect them to be straight with me. This is the only way to get things sorted out. Most of the players are happy here and I treat them all the same."

It was Spavin's turn next. He sent a detailed open letter to the LEP to explain to the fans exactly what had happened appearing under the headline, **'I'M SORRY TO GO LIKE THIS!'**

I'M SORRY TO GO LIKE THIS!

ALAN SPAVIN, the man in the middle of the crisis at Deepdale, today hit out at the comments made by Preston caretaker manager Frank Lord yesterday and the board's handling of North End affairs:

In a letter to the "Lancashire Evening Post," he says:

I'VE READ with dismay the allegations made by Frank Lord re my departure from Deepdale, and would be obliged if you could put my feelings in print so that at least people can be left to judge for themselves whether I'm guilty of rocking the boat as accused.

I will begin by saying that my argument with the club has nothing whatever to do with my being left out of the side and, in fact, when told I was to be dropped, my very words were that I could not grumble as I had not been playing well.

It is in treatment received thereafter that the bitterness had emerged.

I spent three-and-a-half weeks going into training at Deepdale without a word being spoken to me by Frank Lord.

I was left out of all first team squad training sessions and completely disregarded in so many ways

Along with this, many other incidents occurred involving other players and, in fact, staff as well, which I could not comprehend or believe. This made me feel totally dejected and I became so angry that I saw the chairman on Thursday, March 15th, gave him my views and asked the board to consider termination of my contract.

Also on this day, I ceased to go to Deepdale for training until my position was clarified.

I formally made a repeat of my request by letter to the board exactly one week ago, but am still waiting to hear officially from the club. myself.

If I am required to do so, I'm prepared to give detailed descriptions of events previously described, but would prefer that people involved remain anonymous to avoid embarrassment and would clarify this by adding that I've been offered a substantial sum of money by a national newspaper to give my views on the present situation at PNE.

I'm not prepared to do this but would reconsider if I felt it would clear the accusations made against me. I would like to add that I've been at Preston about 16 years, and, in that time, can count on one hand any disputes I've had with them, so I can hardly be accused of being a troublemaker.

Thus I would hope that people might realise how angry I feel at the way affairs have been conducted just recently.

I will close by giving my very best wishes to all the lads and apologising to them if I caused them any embarrassment.

I'm sorry to have to say goodbye to them like this, but feel that, in the circumstances, there is no other way.

I'd like them to know that I'll still be watching them whenever possible and hoping for a good result.

I'd also like to say cheerio to the training staff and office staff, among whom I've made some very good friends.

Also to all PNE supporters whether they be for or against me and to members of The "Lancashire Evening Post" staff who I've come to know so well. Lets hope beter times are ahead.

Lord wac very angry when told of the letter this afternoon, but did not want to contiue what he described as a "slanging match."

"My job is to try to help the club get a few more points," he added.

Meanwhile, Northern Premier Leaguers, Morecambe, say they would jump at the chance of having Spavin on their books, but, because PNE have retained his registration, they cannot make an approach for him unless they were offering a big transfer fee by NPL standards.

The Shrimps' chairman Mr Harry Baines said: "Any club would be foolish not to have an interest in Spavin. He would do a lot of good — especially to us. If there was any chance of him coming to Christie Park, we'd jump at it."

If fact, Morecambe almost made an approach for Spav when he was out of favour shortly after Alan Ball came to Deepdale but were put off by the cash which would have been involved.

Alan Spavin writes to the North End fans via the LEP to explain why he's leaving after 15 years at Deepdale

While all this was going on, eight local businessmen had put together a takeover bid for the club. The news received front page coverage in the LEP. A column by Shakeshaft reported the details, and commended the plan, declaring; *"...the nonsense of the old voting structure will be gone forever."* The aim was to raise £250,000 via a £1 share issue, and to start the ball rolling, the consortium would buy 150,000 of them. The remaining 100,000 would go on open sale. Directors would have to purchase a stake of 2,500 shares as a minimum. Voting rights would be on the basis of one share – one vote. Shakeshaft's view was that the directors would never be able to hold their heads high if they turned down the £150,000 offer with the club estimated to be £100,000 in debt.

Besides receiving the LEP backing, the proposal also received the approval of the Deepdale Action Group. Chairman Ross Gallacher said, *"We hope the directors will do the right thing for the good of the club and resign to make way for the new men. They say they have the future of the club at heart, but it is obvious they have not been able to provide the leadership necessary for North End to be improved – and we deplore the mishandling of the Alan Spavin affair. A loyal servant has been lost to the club, and North End have only themselves to blame for the bad publicity which has again brought them into disrepute."*

Meanwhile North End travelled to Brighton to play the bottom club in Division Two on the last day of March. All hopes were dashed as another poor performance resulted in a 2-0 defeat, and saw North End drop another two places down the ladder to 18th position.

"WE'RE SET TO QUIT SAY DIRECTORS – Let's see your money" shouted the LEP headline in the April 4th edition. The takeover bid seemed to be going in a positive direction; although it was clear there were still pockets of resistance on the North End Board. Shakeshaft went through the issues for the readers.

"The bid is the best ever made, but if the board can come up with a better suggestion, the directors would be justified in refusing.

Take-over bid for North End

EIGHT Lancashire business and professional men have come forward with a quarter of a million pounds scheme to save Preston North End.

They propose that the present directors should resign to make way for them on the board and that there should be a complete re-organisation of the company's structure.

To bring this about, they plan to issue 200,000 new shares at £1 each and say they are prepared to take up the first 150,000 of these in their own contributions and from promises already received.

The eight men have been working towards their aims for several weeks, and one of their members, Mr Tom Croft, the chairman of the Croft Group of companies, and a county councillor, is the PNE shareholder who originally put forward a [illegible]

The eight men who want to take control

Mr Leeming · Mr Eaves · Mr Croft · Mr Johnson
Mr McCann · Mr Bridges · Mr Wade · Mr Edmundson

[illegible] cluding our own personal contributions, we anticipate being able to take up 150,000 shares.

(iii) The share qualification of each director shall be the holding of at least 2,500 shares and any director co-opted would be required to take up this minimum holding.

(iv) Consider in detail other proposals which we have informally discussed but with which we cannot progress without further information and all relevant facts.

We have no dispute with individual members of the present board — many of whom are known to certain of us. However, knowing also of your concern for the future of North End and having in mind your often quoted comment that this is the directors' sole concern, we expect — and the public will expect — you all to do "the right thing" for the club and resign.

Having stated our position privately in this statement, we intend, however, to make our proposals public knowledge.

Let's see your money — directors

WE'RE SET TO QUIT SAY PNE BOARD

By NORMAN SHAKESHAFT

THE "TAKEOVER" bid for Preston North End has been given a provisional go-ahead by the board of directors.

After meeting for more than six hours last night, in three sessions, they finally agreed to accept the proposals made by the eight Lancashire business and professional men, last week, if the £150,000 mentioned by the consortium can be deposited for the club —and providing the board cannot raise a similar amount in the meantime.

The statement

"Following a meeting held on April 3rd between the signatories of the letter addressed to the board of directors and the board, it was resolved that, when the sum of £150,000 has been deposited with a bank for the benefit of Preston North End Football Club Limited, the board will then be prepared to accept the proposals put forward, provided, in the meantime, the board do not raise a similar amount. In the event of Article 5 of the Articles of Association not being amended by the shareholders at an extraordinary general meeting to permit one vote for each share held, then the signatories shall be released from their obligation."

The ball is therefore back in the court of Mr Tom Croft, and his seven colleagues, but they anticipate no difficulty in complying with the board's request and it looks as if they may well be in charge at Deepdale in the near future, with the present directors resigning to make way for them.

Mr Croft is away on business today, but Mr Bob Wade, said, on behalf of the takeover group, that they were "generally optimistic" and that they would be giving an answer to the board within the next few days.

Afterwards Mr David Eaves, one of them, said, again on behalf of them all: "We welcome the statement issued by the Board this morning and are obliged to them for the kind invitation to attend their meeting last night. We are reviewing the various aspects of the situation and a further statement will be issued as soon as possible."

In fact, seven of the men [illegible]

MR. NICHOLSON

Preston this afternoon, and their plans are going ahead. Their representatives had been met by the directors in [illegible] sions last night, when questions were asked by the board.

The directors then met once more in private before a statement was made by Mr Tom Nicholson, the North End chairman this morning.

The statement is scrupulously fair and is a credit to the nine directors and especially Mr Nicholson, who has undoubtedly had the difficult task of bringing both sides of the board together.

The members who have said in the past few days that they would fight the takeover still have the chance to try to raise more than £150,000 in the next few days and it could only be for the good of the club, if they came up with a new, superior alternative.

But their opportunity of doing this looks very slim and they are now committed [illegible]

[illegible] tors in favour of the proposals if their efforts fail and if the £150,000 is deposited satisfactorily.

The agreement reached last night was not a definite resolution, but it is as near to one as could be expected in the circumstances, with the directors having a responsibility to ensure that the £150,000 is available before stepping down to co-opt their eight successors.

But, although only two of them are likely to be brought back to keep continuity, they have all shown quite clearly that they have the club at heart as they have always said, and which has never been disputed.

The new men who now look likely to have the task of building a brighter future for North End say they have raised the £150,000 from personal contributions, and from promises already made.

The takeover offer is placed before the board but was eventually rejected…and the status quo maintained

"If there is no superior alternative, then surely they have to make way for the new men – if they have the club at heart as they have always insisted.

"There are suggestions from the board that the £150,000 may not be available, but Mr Croft and his associates refute this completely and will show them the colour of their money at a moment's notice.

"The directors can throw the plan out of course, for any scheme that hasn't the backing of the board would be defeated at an existing shareholders meeting. The present voting rights ensure this for the directors to have a tight grip, explaining why the club has been accused of being a closed shop."

Within little more than a week, the board refused to resign despite holding a meeting with the consortium. The deal was effectively dead in the water.

Shakeshaft reported : *"A board meeting last night considered all sides of the situation and the consortium members were spoken to afterwards. PNE chairman, Tom Nicholson said avoiding relegation was the priority at the moment, and it was in everyone's interest that no change was made at this vital time."*

The board issued a long an rambling statement, but the key element surrounded the 'readily available' £150,000. The board wouldn't accept the written statement that Mr Aldred, Natwest Bank Manager, Fishergate, had before him, *"...evidence that leaves me to state that the sum of £150,000 would be available for the purchase of 150,000 one pound shares in Preston North End FC."*

The board's response was the final nail in the consortium's coffin... *"...and in view of the fact that £150,000 has not actually deposited in the bank account, the board have by a majority vote, withdrawn the pledge given on April 3rd to accept the proposals outlined."*

The consortium officially withdrew their offer a few days later, feeling that the North End Board had been generally obstructive.

In the meantime, PNE chairman Tom Nicholson made a statement of his own about the situation – completely disassociating himself from the board's decision not to resign. *"…I have always considered that the lifeline should be grasped, and endeavoured during the discussions to reach an amicable settlement. Personal aggrandisement has had no part of my association with PNE and I am concerned only with its welfare and success.*

"The statement made by the board last week did not have my support."

It was all very intriguing, but unfortunately the 'lifeline ship' had already sailed. It did indicate, however, perhaps just why some of the other incumbent directors occupied their places at the boardroom table.

Around the time of the Brighton defeat, and amid all the board politics and general woe, a report in the LEP by Blackpool FC correspondent Stanley Whittaker had the North End fans reaching for the tranquilisers again.

Bruce—Blackpool transfer target?

SECRET transfer talks between near-neighbours Blackpool and Preston North End are thought to have reached the advanced stage arising from the Seasiders' bidding for Alex Bruce, the talented young Deepdale sharpshooter (writes STANLEY WHITTAKER).

At Bloomfield - road today, however, manager Harry Potts refused to comment.

It suggested that Blackpool were in advanced negotiations to lift Alex Bruce out of the North End carnage in a cash plus player deal. The youngster, in his first real lengthy run of first team appearances had caught everybody's eye with his determined attitude to put the ball in the net. He was the hope for the future that we fans were clinging to. Surely the board could see the ire that would run through the fan base if they went through with such a move? Thankfully, they did – and realised that connecting with clubs over Bruce was surely playing with fire.

Control and the effective policy of Preston North End had obviously stayed with the bank, as focus returned to the field for the nerve wracking ending to the season.

After a 0-0 draw at home to Huddersfield, North End checked in at Bloomfield Road for the local derby. Another defeat was registered; beaten 2-0 in a match that saw Alan Kelly stretchered off the pitch and Hugh McIlmoyle heroically take over between the sticks.

It all made for interesting television in Sunday lunchtime's 'Kick-Off Match,' but North End were still winless since Lord took over as caretaker manager, and now stood 19th – with just a three point cushion between themselves and the teams occupying the relegation places. One of those teams, Cardiff City had two games in hand over North End.

Midweek brought the news that Clive Clark had been suspended by the club over a breach of discipline. The winger had repeatedly failed to report for training, citing reasons of discontent with his situation at the club. Known to have been an open supporter of sacked manager Ball, he hadn't been near the first team since the March 17th defeat at Millwall. It was understood he was following Spavin's example and asking for his cards. It was a sad end, for 'Chippy' Clark never gave less than 100% for North End and was a player of some quality. Alex Spark had also registered his desire to leave, which just about knocked on the head any lingering suggestions that Ball had ever 'lost the team.'

Four games left and the Easter programme opened with a home fixture against Nottingham Forest. A crowd of 7,701 witnessed the first Preston win of 1973, by 2-1. It was a vast improvement upon what North End had been serving up in recent times, with goals from Neil Young and

Bruce sealing the win, against a Forest team that included rising star Duncan McKenzie and former North End favourite, George Lyall.

Easter Monday saw a trek down the M5 to Ashton Gate, home of Bristol City. There was little that could be described as 'positive' that emerged out of this game for the Lilywhites, as they were predictably put to the sword by 2-1; the pundits advising that it could have been a far wider margin.

Still in 19th place, the following evening saw the conclusion of the holiday programme with a crucial match at home to Oxford United. Popular opinion suggested that North End could probably avoid the dreaded trap door if they managed to glean just a point from the contest. A gift goal handed to the visitors in the 15th minute was enough to settle the issue however, in a match that saw very little quality emanate from the home side. The very slow exit from the field by the North End players at the final whistle didn't need any explaining.

And so to the last game of this traumatic season – a derby game at Deepdale against champions-elect Burnley. Win or draw, and it's survival. Lose, and barring a permutation miracle, North End are relegated.

The scene was set.

CHAPTER 10

1972/73

PRESTON NORTH END V BURNLEY
APRIL 28TH 1973

Bruce delivers salvation

I must confess I was an avid North End programme collector back in my school days. I loved to read them from cover to cover, and keep them in as near mint condition as possible.

The Burnley game was no different. I bought the programme from the bloke near the Pavilion Stand car park, and walked around to the Town End turnstiles. Once through, my nose was straight in it, as I progressed to my spot at the back of the stand – as always only looking downwards from the pages occasionally to make sure my footing was secure.

As I approached the top of the stand, I looked up and John caught my eye. Motioning to behind me he said, with a laugh in his voice, "Seen that bloody lot out theer?!" Puzzled, I turned around. It took me a second or two to grasp what he was getting so animated about...then I saw it! The touchlines had been moved in on both sides by at least six feet and the pitch had puddles all over it – strange as this had been a dry, bright but cool spring day so far.

"Why?" I asked myself – of course it was to nullify the threat of the Burnley wingers – the brilliant Leighton James in particular – and bring the game into the middle. I looked back at John and said, "I take it its allowed?" at which another bloke chimed in, "Aye, lad, as long as the pitch is within the limits. They drenched the pitch an'all so it's slippy."

One thing immediately struck me...the sheer desperation North End had apparently slumped to under the stewardship of Frank Lord since the sacking of Alan Ball. I suppose the view was that the team had blown so many gilt edged opportunities to grasp safety in the weeks before, that everything possible to assist within the rules was going to be utilised this final time.

The North End team for this very last throw of the dice was:-

Kelly, McMahon, Snookes, Bird, Hawkins, Baxter (S), Connor, Bruce, Lamb, Spark and Young. Substitute: McIlmoyle

North End emerged first, and immediately formed a guard of honour to applaud Burnley on to the pitch in recognition of their promotion to Division One. They had enjoyed a fine season, and had a very slick team made up of 75% talented youth, and 25% good old experienced pro's who occupied key positions. They were managed by former captain Jimmy Adamson, a likeable chap, who had said the previous evening on Granada's 'Kick Off' preview show, that he had sympathy for all at North End but he hoped Burnley would win 4-0. It was delivered with a smile and tongue firmly in cheek!

I recall marvelling at North End's formation as they took position at kick off. It wasn't the fact that they lined up in a very defensive formation, it was more the fact of just who was playing where! John McMahon, Stuart Baxter, John Bird and Eric Snookes comprised the back four, with Dave Connor, Alex Spark, Graham Hawkins and Neil Young in midfield. Alex Bruce and Alan Lamb would be the front runners. Hawkins in midfield? Really??

A big roar of anticipation greeted the kick-off, with Burnley attacking the Kop. The wall of sound was supplied largely by the huge amount of Burnley fans present in the large 21,550 crowd, sited in large pockets all around the ground.

The visitors were quickly into their stride, with the pattern of play established early; Burnley on all-out attack, North End defending.

Kelly had to make a good diving save from James early on, after Frank Casper had flicked on a Jim Thompson through ball. The ball ran loose but Snookes had no hesitation in booting it behind for a corner. North End were pinned in their own half and being worked very hard – albeit in a much narrower playing area, which hadn't seemed to quieten James down at all. In fact, he was all over North End like a rash, pushing the ball slowly forward to the defenders with his right foot, then accelerating past them like Billy Whizz.

Judging by the noise, the Burnley fans on the Kop were convinced that a 25 yard screamer from James was goal bound – but it veered past the angle of post and crossbar at the last moment. North End simply had no forward motion at this point – the activity areas of the game were there for all to see; a cut up, well worn North End half, and largely untouched green Burnley pasture!

By now Hawkins and Connor were retreating back into defence whenever needed, as a mass of white shirts defended Kelly's goal. This would have been quite understandable in the normal scheme of things if we were five minutes from time, but there was still 20 minutes left of the first half!

North End hearts sank when every Burnley attacker plus the thousands on the Kop shouted for a penalty when Baxter stopped the ball in the area, but the referee carried on running and waving play on as the ball was hoofed out of play towards the half way line.

Lamb and Bruce were rarely in the game, as the North End defence were seemingly too panic stricken to use them as an outlet, preferring to kick the ball into the crowd to relieve the pressure.

A Paul Fletcher header from a James centre tested Kelly next, but the Irishman held onto the ball following his low dive to the right. Next, a Doug Collins 20 yarder skimmed the turf heading for the North End goal, but the shot was blocked by Connor; once again taking control of the ball but content to kick the ball away for a throw rather than pass forward and develop a move.

James then powered in a drive from the edge of the box after running in laterally from the left side, which Kelly saved at full stretch and heroically recovered in time to block Casper's follow up attempt too. It was truly watching-through-your-hands-time for the North End fans!

By now, Martin Dobson – a midfielder with some degree of class – was pulling the Burnley strings. North End, or should I say caretaker manager Lord, needed to cut off the supply to him somehow but continued instead with the tactics of sitting back and defending for their lives. It wasn't very pretty...but it was about to become stunningly beautiful!

Burnley, with all their claret shirts in attack mode, saw another North End clearing punt hurtle in the direction of midfielder Billy Ingham, just within the North End half. He made a hash of an attempted headed pass and the ball fell instead to Lamb, who quickly took the ball forward into the Burnley half. Racing clear by now he was tracked by Bruce to his right and former England full back Keith Newton who was caught between the North End pair. The roar and screams of anticipation now belonged to the North End fans as the two youngsters progressed to the edge of the Burnley penalty area.

Lamb chose his moment well to square the ball to Bruce around 15 yards out from goal, and with Newton scrambling across towards him and goal keeper Alan Stevenson helplessly exposed the new North End hero buried a low hard drive into the back of the net without any hesitation whatsoever. Unbelievably, this was the first goal Burnley had conceded in six games!

Wild celebrations in the crowd and indeed on the pitch had barely subsided when the referee decided it was time for a cup of tea and blew for half time.

Alex Bruce drills home the ball to give North End the lead...

...and celebrates in style!

It was a blessing that the ball had fallen to Bruce to execute the goal. In all his 30 matches of this particular season (this was his 13th goal), the youngster had never flinched in any situation he had found himself in. I have mentioned before that as far as scoring was concerned this lad played without fear, so confident was he in his ability. If there was anything to come out of this expectant season that had so tragically turned sour, it was the emergence of Bruce who would in time, quite rightly, assume the mantle of a North End legend.

Lord obviously hadn't heard the half time discussion around my vantage point on the Town End – largely of the viewpoint that North End wouldn't get away with another half like that again and had to pose Burnley some problems.

The second half began, and the activity was once again exclusively in the now greener North End half. A Collins free kick was curled into the North End goalmouth and caused real anxiety as the ball bounced around and the North End fans screamed at the defence to clear the ball. Eventually it was.

Next, James swung a corner in from the left and Fletcher rose high to power a header that beat Kelly, only to see Snookes clear off the line. The signs were ominous, and Burnley finally broke through in the 54th minute with the equaliser they quite frankly deserved.

A quickly taken throw by Casper on the left was flicked on by Dobson to the edge of the North End box where Colin Waldron headed the ball onwards into the centre of the area. Nulty and Bird contested for the ball which looped back towards Waldron who caught the ball perfectly on the volley to blast the ball back and into the North End net, with the diving Kelly still airborne.

This time it was the turn of the thousands of Burnley fans to roar their approval, as we North End fans all looked at each other. "Bloody hell – that's put tin hat on it," said John shaking his head as though we were witnessing the last life breaths of someone dying. It was hard to argue the point as North End had shown little interest in going forward and creating anything. The impetus had been with the Clarets since the first whistle. Now buoyed, they came back for more.

The visitors passing became even sharper and crisper than before, as they injected more speed into their forward movement. They were on fire, with shots raining in on Kelly's goal from all angles. Baxter was then booked for hacking James down when he was almost clean through and the resulting free kick from Collins went inches over the bar.

Eventually, just like the sun after a very rainy day, North End pushed their noses out of their own half – and found that it wasn't half as dreadful as they had imagined. This was good; besides eating up time, Burnley were not a threat if North End had the ball in the visitors half.

During this interlude of Preston attacks, a left foot cross from Young wreaked havoc as it travelled across the heart of the Burnley goalmouth with players of both teams hacking at the ball. It was finally Spark who connected with the ball, but the Scot screwed his shot wide of the right hand post.

Burnley breezed forward again, but McMahon stood his ground and stole the ball as James came marauding down the flank towards him. This won applause from the home crowd, which turned into roars as the full back passed the ball forward down the right to Lamb, in space. Down the wing he went, releasing the ball infield to Young whose centre found Bruce who headed just wide.

As the minutes were being anxiously counted down, the game slowed down with both teams seemingly content with what they had – but then Burnley laid siege to North End's goal one more time.

Twice Kelly was called upon to save amid a mixture of cries of relief and anguish from the home supporters. His second save I will never forget; as James pulled back his right foot only six yards from goal, Kelly threw himself at the Welshman's feet to claim the ball – and a thud in the ribs too. So brave, so Alan Kelly.

This was the day that Kelly became the new league appearance record holder for North End – and what a performance he had saved for the occasion! He was called upon one more time as, with the whistles from the North End fans resonating around the ground, Dobson launched an almighty drive towards goal. The shot was only partially saved by the sprawling keeper, but thankfully cleared well away from near the goal line by Connor.

The final whistle blew, and Deepdale was invaded by the younger element of the masses from Burnley. The pitch occupancy lasted quite a while, and both the North End crossbars were broken in the general misbehaviour. The home fans had long sidled off home however, happy with the humblest of gifts – a solitary league point that guaranteed Division Two safety.

Deepdale deliverance

ALEX BRUCE

Preston players applaud Division 2 leaders Burnley on to the pitch

BRUCE KEEPS PRESTON SAFE!

THE MIRACLE happened at Deepdale today when Preston held on for a 1-1 draw against Burnley to take the point which keeps them in the Second Division next season.

By NORMAN SHAKESHAFT

The result was a slight disappointment to Burnley who would have created a new away points record if they won, but the draw ensured that they will be promoted to the First Division as Second Division champions.

"A great goal to score, not a brilliant goal but a very important goal," was how Alex Bruce latterly recalled his strike that ensured North End's Division Two status was retained in 1973.

This wasn't quite the end of things in 1972/73 for the North End fan. Just two days after the Burnley game, a boardroom reshaping took place as Tom Nicholson, Allan Harrison and Tom Charnley all tendered their resignations. They were replaced by Gerald Brown, Michael Johnson and local millionaire businessman, Trevor Hemmings.

The PNE Board now consisted: Alan Jones (chairman), Trevor Hemmings (vice-chairman), and Messers Bolton, Brown, Gore, Griffith, Johnson, Wilde and Pilkington.

Graham Hawkins takes a refreshing swig from a bottle of Burnley's champagne after North End's survival

A 'cash injection' accompanied the changes, in the form of guarantees to the bank. Each member pledged £10,000 with Hemmings a further £60,000 to underpin an overdraft facility now set at £150,000. The Bank would only call upon the money if the company failed. The directors would adopt their new *'Forward Policy'*, the first objective being the survival of league football in Preston. The second was to retain or sign players of as high a standard as the club could afford without prejudicing its survival. The club was to be seen strictly in business terms, and was to be kept under stringent financial control.

The news received a guarded welcome from LEP correspondent Norman Shakeshaft, who hoped it would eventually bring about the transformation needed. In the event, the terms *'as high a standard as the club could afford'* and *'under stringent financial control'* didn't look much different from the previous administration's *mode d'emploi*.

Two days further on from all that news, the national newspapers broke the sensational story that Bobby Charlton had been approached by the new North End Board with a view to appointing him as their new manager.

Charlton had ended his glittering Manchester United career at Stamford Bridge, Chelsea on the same day that North End had escaped relegation by the skin of their teeth at Deepdale by gaining that all-important point against Burnley. It certainly set the town talking, and Charlton delivered his positive decision to the board a few days later.

A 'reshaped' board, Bobby Charlton as manager, and the new chairman stating, *"We are all in this together."* What could possibly go wrong?

Preston go for Charlton

BOBBY CHARLTON has been offered the chance of restoring the long-lost glamour of Preston North End. The man who played his last game of football last night confirmed that the Second Division club has asked him to become their manager.

From DAVID BARNES in VERONA

The Manchester United star has told them he will give his decision by the weekend.

The Preston offer is only one of several approaches from clubs anxious to link Charlton's famous name to theirs.

Minutes before his final appearance in the red shirt of United he admitted: 'Yes, Preston have asked me if I would like to manage them.

'I am very embarrassed that this has come out before I am ready to make up my mind.

'There are other clubs involved. I don't want to say who they are. But what division any club is in will make no difference to what I decide.'

I understand that Preston have made the only managerial offer. The others are more interested in Charlton to pass on his vast playing experience as a coach. Ironically, the other main runner for the Deepdale job is Charlton's former boss at Old Trafford, Frank O'Farrell.

The plunge for Charlton is a blow to Frank Lord, who has wrestled with relegation problems since Preston fired manager Alan Ball three months ago.

Preston desperately need a new, ambitious thrust to let them share in the boom of Lancashire's town clubs. They clearly see Charlton as the perfect impetus in that drive for success.

So next season could be one of intense rivalry between Charlton and his brother, Jack.

With the Leeds United centre half lining up a new future in charge of Middlesbrough they could be in direct opposition.

CHAPTER 11

1973/74

PRESTON NORTH END V WEST BROMWICH ALBION
OCTOBER 1ST 1973

The 'New North End' take to the field...

As a result of hiring the services of Bobby Charlton (official start date June 1st 1973), the goings on at Deepdale were never out of the news – not just the local news either; Charlton brought access to column space in the national press that North End hadn't enjoyed since the Finney era. Season ticket sales were well up on previous years, and so were the enquiries regarding stadia advertising around the Deepdale pitch perimeter. All in the garden was rosy, and the 1972/73 season fast becoming a distant memory.

The first item on the new manager's agenda was to entice Alan Spavin back to the club he had served so well. *"He's now very keen to play for us again and all the problems that existed before have now been sorted out,"* said Charlton, adding *"the club and the player are both very happy with the situation."*

Next, Charlton secured the services of his former Manchester United team mate, Francis Burns, who was looking for a move back north after failing to settle after his move to Southampton from Manchester United. This was all positive and to really set things alight, Charlton and his charges just needed to engineer a flying start to the season. Alas, life wasn't meant to be that easy...

After an indifferent pre-season tour of Scotland, North End began in earnest with an away fixture at Villa Park August 25th. Some North End fans travelled in style to the game, as North End with their new found fame, were granted first use in the new season of the novel 'League Liner' for their highly hopeful followers.

The Villa match attracted the full attention of the media, was covered in all the Sunday and daily papers and by local Midlands ITV company ATV for their Sunday afternoon television programme, 'Star Soccer'. Alas the result didn't match the new high expectations, as North End capitulated to two late Villa goals, after spending most of the game just about 'hanging in.'

North End 'under the cosh' in the first league game of Bobby Charlton's regime as Aston Villa's Brian Little powers in a shot

Eager to improve his team Charlton convinced his brother Jack, manager of Middlesbrough, to sell him Nobby Stiles, the no-nonsense ex

Manchester United and England half back two days later for a £20,000 fee. It would mark the beginning of a long association between Stiles and North End, one that fans of a certain age will never forget.

An eventual League Cup defeat after a Deepdale replay at the hands of Bolton Wanderers, followed by a home draw against Swindon Town and a defeat at Hull City in the league, saw North End languish in 21st position in Division Two. The edge had certainly been taken off the big summer build-up to this campaign by now, but things were suddenly to get better... much better.

Thankfully, North End would win five of their next eight Division Two fixtures. The run started on September 11th with a midweek home win over Millwall by 2-0, followed by a 1-1 draw at home to Bristol City – the unfortunate Alan Kelly dislocating a shoulder – a fantastic 0-2 away win at The Hawthorns against much fancied West Bromwich Albion, a 1-1 draw at the City Ground against Forest and a 2-1 home win against Porstmouth on September 29th. This welcome run pushed North End up to a very respectable eighth in the Division Two table.

The return fixture against West Bromwich Albion came around very quickly due to some peculiarity in the league computer, which had spat out the Deepdale game as October 1st. It was to be a match to remember – arguably the peak performance of Charlton's tenure.

I was in my first job by now, and after a day's work was finding out how physically tiring it all was – most nights I was snoring away an hour or so after tea! I had managed to see all of North End's home games to date, and wasn't going to miss this game after sensing that the team were finally playing with some potential.

Burns had impressed me most of all Charlton's signings; he really did look like a Division One player, demonstrating vision, passing accuracy and coolness under pressure. Stiles had slotted in well too, he didn't run around much, he let the ball do all that for him via the use of intelligent passing usually after recovering the ball for his team.

My mum thrust a flask of coffee at me soon after tea, remembering I had mentioned that I was so tired I hoped that I would keep awake during the game! "Here, take this with you – just don't fall asleep on the bus on the way home!"

I recall it being a balmy sort of evening and hoping to change North End's luck at the start of the season, had changed my vantage point again. I was now in the Pavilion Paddock towards the back, near where the terracing was fenced off next to the Town End....approximately in line with the penalty spot.

Deepdale was buzzing that night and with over 15,000 present, it was as though the fans were slowly emerging from their shelters and starting to believe that there might just be something happening under Bobby Charlton after all.

North End took the field with a debutant on board, 19 year old Gordon Coleman. He had been called into action as Charlton's preferred centre forward, Mel Holden, had picked up an ankle injury during the home win over Portsmouth a few days earlier. Alex Spark came into the team, replacing Alan Lamb, also suffering from an ankle injury. Young winger Gary Williams retained his position warming the bench. The North End team was:-

Brown, McMahon, McNab, Baxter (S), Hawkins, Stiles, Spark, Burns, Coleman, Bruce, Young. Sub: Williams

Play from the start was fast and furious from North End who, attacking the Town End, were obviously intent on denting the visitors prospects from the word 'go.' Neat passing and slick movement brought applause from the home fans with relegated Albion chasing shadows.

After seven minutes, North End won a free kick down the right, near the visitor's penalty area. Neil Young swung a curling ball into the goalmouth and the three nearest candidates, West Brom's Gordon Nisbett and goalkeeper Peter Latchford along with Francis Burns of North End contested the ball.

Burns seemed to wrap his outstretched leg around Nisbett and poke the ball past the diving Latchford; all three participants ending in a bundle watching the ball, along with the expectant crowd, trickle into the corner of the net.

Francis Burns prods the ball into the net from behind the WBA defender

While Deepdale erupted with joy, Asa Hartford took it upon himself to chase the referee back to the centre circle and vehemently argue the case for a foul. Only when Mr Lee finally brandished his book did the blonde haired midfielder rapidly withdraw from the 'conversation.'

Play continued as before; North End well on top and keeping their nerve. Five minutes later, there was more commotion between the Albion players and the referee as North End doubled their lead in sensational style.

Burns collected a pass and progressed down the right before crossing the ball into the penalty area. The ball was headed well clear by big John Wile, the Albion centre half and captain as Young and Coleman challenged.

Nobody in the ground that night – players or fans – could believe what happened next!

As everybody's eyes followed the looping ball to about 30 yards from Latchford's goal line, it was suddenly met with an almighty swing of the airborne John McMahon's boot that sent the ball screaming in one devastating second into the back of the West Brom net. It was an incredible strike!

Mr Lee awarded the goal and set off for the centre circle amid the din from the crowd. Exuberance was tempered however; he was immediately surrounded by the West Brom players pointing to the linesman still holding his flag aloft, the issue seemingly being McMahon's missile hadn't given Young and Coleman enough time to get back onside.

John McMahon's 30 yard volley flies high into the net before the goalkeeper can react

We needn't have bothered. The referee waved aside his linesman's flag, clarifying after the game, that the North End pair, *"were not interfering with play and couldn't possibly have done so in the time it took the ball to travel directly into the net from the Preston players' boot."*

North End remained on top for the rest of the half, with Nobby Stiles in particular reveling in his recently acquired role as North End captain. He brought a unique snarling bite to midfield that North End had never enjoyed before. It wasn't all about his bossy competiveness though; Stiles could play football.

Charlton had handed the notorious half back the captains role five matches previously, arguing that the responsibility of the role was affecting the performance of Graham Hawkins. If that was the real reason for the transfer of command, I had never noticed it and doubt anybody else had! However, North End were unbeaten in this period, so who could argue?

The first half ended with a flurry of West Brom attacks, none of which had any real defence piercing quality. John Brown, the North End goalkeeper had enjoyed a quiet 45 minutes generally and it was from his drop kick that Mr Lee blew for half time.

The half time chatter was all about the North End goals. The one comment that has stuck with me was from an elderly chap who had obviously been watching North End for a very long time. He said, *"I have never – NEVER – seen a ball driven in like that in all my life before..."* He was of course talking about McMahon's shot, North End's second goal. As I write, it is 45 years on from that time, and I am more than happy to repeat those just as relevant words today!

Play resumed and North End weren't for sitting back on their lead. In fact it took only five minutes for them to totally kill off any hopes of an Albion revival.

A neat passage of play initially involving both Stiles and Coleman, saw the ball threaded forward to Young. Gathering pace whilst playing a one-two with Burns, Young took a few more strides forward and just into the visitors penalty area whereupon he unleashed a terrific right foot shot that curled around Latchford before nestling in the bottom left corner of his net.

This now made the transfer listed midfielder North End's leading goalscorer with four goals. On days like this the enigmatic Young was an undeniable asset; the problem seemed to be that there were just not enough of these type of days! That wasn't my thought at the time though – I was celebrating another superbly crafted and executed North

End goal with the rest of the crowd.

Two views of North End's third goal taken at the same moment. Neil Young arcs the ball around the WBA goalkeeper to seal victory

As time rolled on, Coleman increasingly caught the eye, and many of the crowd were impressed with what they saw. He seemed to be playing the centre forward role as a direct replacement for the tall target man Holden, but he was much more mobile, was blessed with a deft touch and very aware of space for someone so young. It wasn't a surprise to me that when he eventually broke permanently into the team he became a midfielder – and a very good one too!

An injury to Jim McNab who left the field with what turned out to be a thigh injury saw a mini reshuffle. Alex Spark fell back from midfield to cover the now vacant left back role, with the substitute, young Gary Williams taking his place on the left side of midfield.

With 20 minutes still remaining that superb striker, Tony Brown finally pulled a goal back for the 'Baggies.' Hartford moved down the right hand side and crossed the ball quickly into the North End box to meet the run of Alistair Brown, who headed the ball down and directly into the path of his namesake, who swept the ball home without breaking stride.

As good a goal as this was, it served as little more than to keep West Brom's interest in affairs alive for the remainder of the game, as a North End win was never in doubt.

With the two points secured, North End leapt from eighth to second place and once more in the topsy-turvy Seventies, Deepdale was bursting with high hopes.

After the game, Albion manager Don Howe bemoaned the fact to the press that he didn't have a 'Nobby Stiles' he could rely on to control things in midfield. West Brom certainly lacked that type of inspiration and Howe's comments were in effect, a fitting tribute to the Preston skipper.

Desperate WBA manager Don Howe cries out for a Nobby Stiles

PRESTON RIDING HIGH!

TELL-TALE TABLE

	P	W	D	L	F	A	Pts.
Middlesbrough	8	4	3	1	7	4	11
Preston	9	4	3	2	12	8	11
Bristol City	8	5	1	2	10	7	11
Luton Town	7	4	2	1	17	10	10
Fulham	8	3	4	1	6	4	10
Bolton	7	4	1	2	7	3	9
Nottingham For.	8	3	3	2	12	7	9
Orient	8	2	5	1	10	7	9
Aston Villa	8	2	5	1	8	6	9
Notts County	8	4	1	3	13	12	9

CHAPTER 12

1973/74

PRESTON NORTH END V SUNDERLAND
OCTOBER 13TH 1973

Another fantastic win….

Following the superb win over West Bromwich Albion, North End travelled to Fulham who like the Lilywhites were flying high in Division Two. Nobody was really surprised when the teams cancelled each other out; both teams settling for a goalless draw.

North End next entertained mighty Sunderland. I say 'mighty' as at that time they were the FA Cup holders and favourites to be promoted to Division One. They had beaten Leeds United at Wembley – back then arguably the best team in the United Kingdom – in one of the biggest footballing 'turnovers' in the history of the game. They hadn't set Division Two alight just yet however, and sat ninth, two points behind North End in fifth.

Bearing in mind the build up and interest in the match, I headed off towards Deepdale early as there was likely to be a big crowd. I wasn't wrong; 21,747 assembled inside the old ground to witness an epic contest.

The teams marched out to loud cheers: Preston North End v the FA Cup holders! What a prospect this was! Both teams were clad in their classic kits, which added a real sense of history to the occasion.

North End were still beset with injuries, but Bobby Charlton managed to name the following team:-

Brown, McMahon, McNab, Spark, Hawkins, Stiles, Bruce, Young, Coleman, Burns, Williams. Sub: Richmond

North End started the game, attacking the Town End. The formation seemed to indicate that Gordon Coleman, Neil Young and Gary Williams would be furthest forward for North End, with Alex Bruce loitering behind them but in front of midfield.

It was Sunderland who were quickest off the mark though, and could have easily been two goals clear in the first 10 minutes, with a shot from Billy Hughes being blocked and a dangerous run from the left flank by the tricky Dennis Tueart thankfully being terminated by the sure footed tackling of Graham Hawkins. Tueart then appeared on the right, cutting in to beat Jim McNab but pulling his shot well wide of the North End goal. Those were real warning signs, and I'm sure I wasn't the only one wishing that Tueart and his roving role were somewhere else on this particular day!

North End finally retaliated, and following an almighty scramble in front of the Sunderland goal which saw shots from both Coleman and Young blocked, full back Ron Guthrie relieved the pressure by kicking the ball into the mass of Sunderland fans in the Town End.

There was a loud penalty appeal by North End following the corner, as the ball seemed to meet defender David Young's hand as he shaped to control the ball, but the referee, Mr Bosie, disdainfully waved play-on.

North End continued to apply the pressure and were desperately unlucky not to take the lead as half time approached when Coleman set off down the right and launched a wonderful cross on the run towards the unguarded Sunderland back post. With goalkeeper Jim Montgomery off balance as he back pedalled, Williams dashed in quickly from the left side of the box and met the ball square-on; his header smashing into the crossbar and, fortunately for Sunderland, bouncing to safety. Although there was only a near miss to applaud, it did please the fans that two young players who had progressed through the ranks had created such a brilliant opening.

The half came to a close as McNab expertly dispossessed Ian Porterfield – scorer of the Wembley winner – as he made his way into the North End box.

The match had been so engrossing, time had just flown by. Both teams had attacked whenever possible and there was plenty for the crowd to discuss.

It was North End who applied the early pressure upon resumption. A delightful through ball from Nobby Stiles was hit just too firmly for Young to run on to when in the clear and an excellent Hawkins attempt had Montgomery at full stretch as he desperately clung to the defenders' powerful header.

Now it was Sunderland's turn as Tueart drove the ball into the net from close range only to see the linesman with his flag raised for offside against his teammate Billy Hughes. The initial roar of the Wearside fans behind the Town End goal was drowned by the ironic jeers of the North End fans pretty quickly!

North End then really raised the stakes in the 54th minute when they took the lead after the referee awarded them a penalty.

It all began with a line of white shirts moving towards the Kop. Young was to the right, and slid a wonderfully timed ball inside for Bruce to run on to. So good was the pass, it left little for Bruce to do except unleash a

__Top__:

Alex Bruce is floored by a swinging tackle from Ron Guthrie

__Middle__:

The Sunderland protests to the referee drag on and on

__Bottom__

Neil Young makes no mistake from the penalty spot with a thunderbolt drive that gave goalkeeper Jim Montgomery no chance

shot at the Sunderland goal with only Montgomery to beat from 15 yards or so. He did everything right, and drew back his right foot to implement just that. At that point, full back Guthrie crudely hacked him down, taking the youngsters legs from beneath him with a swinging right footed lunge.

A pantomime then followed. How Sunderland could argue and harass the referee in the manner they did and get away with it was ludicrous. Besides the visible anger towards Mr Bosie, I had never witnessed such a stone cold penalty. They were arguing black was white! This went on for approaching two minutes. In this time Young was calmly holding the ball, just walking around the penalty area slowly, looking at the pitch. He was too long in the tooth to be distracted by these shenanigans and so it proved.

When Montgomery finally had the good grace to take his place on the goal line, Young wandered forward and placed the ball on the penalty spot. Every North End fan's heart was pounding a little bit harder as he walked back four or five paces. The Sunderland fans started to whistle loudly from the Town End as Young ran in...and launched a missile that almost took the net of its hooks! Montgomery dived to his right, but Young went straight and slammed the ball into the roof of the net; the ball entering just below the crossbar. Perfect!

As the home crowd acknowledged the goal with loud cheers, Tueart resumed his discussion with Mr Bosie. Upon reaching the half way line, the referee, without saying a word, took his book out and cautioned the winger. That finally shut him up!

Sunderland threw everything forward and once more a golden scoring opportunity for Tueart was denied when Hughes was caught offside at the critical moment. Back they came again, and a Mickey Horswill through ball put the indefatigable Tueart haring through towards John Brown in the North End goal – or so we thought. With the home crowd decibels switched to the setting labelled 'frantic', Hawkins somehow, unbelievably, intercepted with a brilliant last ditch tackle to earn their cheers and appreciation.

With time up and those same North End fans praying and imploring the referee to blow his whistle, the visitors staged one last salvo. It was unbearable!

Following a low hard shot on target by Porterfield that tested Brown's diving skills to the limit, the ball was cleared but only down the middle to Vic Halom, the Sunderland centre forward. He played a quick one-two with Hughes and found himself 10 yards out from goal, just Brown in front of him and the screaming Sunderland fans massed behind. Whether or not that all had an impact on Halom I can't say, but there was just a millisecond of hesitation in his demeanour that gave Brown a vital advantage to position himself and pull off a wonderful point blank save.

Then, finally the whistle blew to loud and prolonged North End cheers. Not a bad day out, you may say, and North End up to third in the table!

Young's penalty blockbuster cracks classy Sunderland

After the game, Young confirmed that he had changed his penalty style for this contest as he knew that Sunderland coach Arthur Cox and Chief Scout Peter Doherty, both ex North End employees, would have instructed goalkeeper Montgomery on his method.

Charlton was a very happy man. *"What a cracking game. It was great to see such a match in front of our best crowd of the season, and wonderful to see us win – and win well."*

Bob Stokoe, however was his usual self. Whether he was like this with all opponents, whether it was because he had previously managed Blackpool or whether it was that he just disliked Preston, I can't say – but he never had a good word to say about North End.

North End's Gordon Coleman under challenge from Sunderland's David Young

Indeed, all he was short of was a big cauldron and a couple of witches by his side as he proclaimed, *"Don't get carried away with Preston's recent successes. You have had it bad for a long time at Deepdale, so enjoy things now while you have the chance."*

If it really was an attempt to curse Preston North End, then he succeeded. From this point on, and for the third season in succession a promising North End campaign would disintegrate into dust...but this time end in relegation to Division Three.

CHAPTER 13

SLIP SLIDING AWAY

Ask any Lilywhite fan about Bobby Charlton's first season in management at North End and sadly it won't be remembered for the stunning entertainment his team provided for the faithful in the autumn of 1973. Instead, the first memory is usually of a decline that eclipsed even those of the previous two seasons, reflected in hesitant performances and meek acceptance of fate as the real tooth and nail scrapping for safety got underway in the spring.

Following the win over Sunderland at Deepdale, North End sat in third position having played 11 games which had returned 14 points, (two points for a win). They finished the season in 21st position having played 42 matches, gaining 31 points. The grim reality is that from the full time whistle on October 13th, North End's record for the remainder of the season was:-

Played 31, Won 4, Drawn 10, Lost 17, Goals for 27, Goals against 54, Points 17 (one point deducted for fielding an ineligible player).

Nobody can argue that relegation isn't assured with that kind of form – and fully deserved if you don't stand up and fight for the cause.

A win against Hull City at Deepdale on December 29th – only the second victory since the home clash with Sunderland – saw North End lie in 15th position with 22 points from 24 games with fans nurturing hopes that the New Year would herald new impetus from both the team and manager. Alas, they would be disappointed as the team fell away at an even greater rate of knots – at one point losing seven out of eight games in the crucial period between the middle of February and the beginning of April, which included a run of five league defeats on the bounce.

Charlton shuffled his team constantly, axed players randomly, and often played established professionals out of position. It really did smack of clutching at straws and was truly awful fare for the fans, now 'shell - shocked' after first being shown the heights of Division Two and then its plunging lows for the third season in a row.

The campaign had seen, unlike with Alan Ball before him, little apparent restraint from the board in terms of supporting Charlton with his needs. He was allowed to bring in Francis Burns, Nobby Stiles, David Sadler, Ray Treacy, Mike Elwiss and a fringe player by the name of David Carrick, who was selected as substitute for the trip to Brunton Park, Carlisle. Alas he wasn't registered with the League in time as North End had thought, and a vital point was duly deducted from North End's tally.

The 'crock of cash' the directors had amassed to back Charlton with when the board reformed earlier in the year must have been close to empty as he discussed his intention with them to bring Elwiss to Deepdale from Doncaster Rovers sometime in January 1974. That's the only possible reason that I can imagine as to why goal machine Alex Bruce was suddenly sold to Newcastle United later in the month for a reported £150,000. Elwiss duly arrived in February.

The Bruce sale was touted by the club to be *'good business'*, *'an offer we couldn't refuse'*, and indeed Charlton's call. The LEP reported, *'...there was a lot of discussion before they reluctantly decided to allow team boss Charlton to sell'.*

Bruce however, did give away a little of his feelings of not being wanted when he said, *"I have always been happy at Deepdale, but I could not refuse to leave when the club were prepared to let me go."*

The cynical North End fans who had seen it all before shook their heads. This was football suicide.

The sale of Bruce was without doubt a massive error. Although he played his last game for North End on January 12th, he still finished the season as the leading goalscorer – in hindsight, Charlton should surely have stood his ground, kept Bruce and demand that the board backed him over Elwiss.

Instead, the board were now behaving as expected and would sell as and when necessary – and only then consider the managers requirements. The die was ominously cast for Charlton when Bruce walked out of the Deepdale door.

At the end of the season, the board pointed out the *'stringent financial situation that faced the club'* and the *'economic necessities'* of life in Division Three to the team manager, and Charlton duly ditched Jim McNab, Neil Young and Eric Snookes, who had all played in the first team during 1973/74. Four reserve team players went too, along with assistant manager Jack Crompton and chief scout Peter Robinson.

Perhaps it was that grim reality that prompted Charlton's next decision...he was to come out of retirement and take to the field again. The revelation certainly had the words 'Preston North End' all over the national media once again, as Charlton was still big news despite his disastrous first season in management. It all made great sense to one colleague at least!

Graham Hawkins: *"When Bobby first arrived and played in the training games during the week, he was still a brilliant player, the best on the field. We asked him repeatedly why he didn't still play. He always said that his days were done but we told him – not in Division Two they aren't! But he wouldn't change his mind."*

BOBBY CHARLTON

Charlton plans a comeback to save his crisis club

BOBBY PLAYS AGAIN

SOCCER hero Bobby Charlton shocked the football world last night by announcing that he is planning a sensational comeback next season.

The retired England star has had an abysmal time in his first season as a manager.

He has seen his club, the once-proud Preston North End—one of the Football League's most famous teams — drop from the Second Division to the Third Division.

His equally-famous brother, Jack, has had a season of unqualified success in his first season as a club boss.

He has taken Middlesbrough from the Second Division to the First.

Now Bobby, 36, will kick off next August as Preston's PLAYER-manager.

His decision to come out of his year-long retirement is not difficult to understand.

EXCLUSIVE By Bob Russell

If that news was the tonic the North End fans needed, the next press release from the club however was an unwelcome dose of North End bitter reality, 1974 vintage.

'The transfer of Graham Hawkins from Preston to Blackburn Rovers was completed at Ewood Park today, for a total fee of £20,000, including the usual percentages.'

North Ender moves in £20,000 deal

● GRAHAM HAWKINS, right, pictured with Blackburn Rovers manager Gordon Lee outside Ewood Park today.

ROVERS SNAP UP HAWKINS

THE transfer of defender Graham Hawkins from Preston to Blackburn was completed at Ewood Park today, for a total fee of nearly £20,000, including the usual percentages.

The 28-year-old player, who was signed by North End from Wolverhampton Wanderers for £35,000 six years ago, signed after talks with Rovers manager Gordon Lee.

I understand that Rovers and Plymouth Argyle, the club managed by Tony Waiters, both made offers for him last week, but that Hawkins was not interested in going to Plymouth. He lives in Lytham and has a garage in Kent-street, Preston, in partnership with former professional boxer Bobby Rhodes.

A 100 per cent. trier, Hawkins has given fine service to Preston, playing in

"I got called into the club in the close season and was told that both Plymouth Argyle and Blackburn Rovers had put bids in for me that the board had accepted – where did I want to go?" Hawkins told me.

"I had no real inkling to go anywhere, but they obviously wanted me to leave. To be fair I wasn't enjoying my football much and couldn't seem to ever really please the management. I was being asked to play in midfield at times which just wasn't me.

"There was no way I was upping sticks and going to Plymouth, so after agreeing it all at home, Rovers it was. It turned out to be a good move for me personally, and Gordon Lee was good to work with. I was back in

the middle of defence, the manager believed in me, we won the Third Division title in 74/75 and I enjoyed my time there."

From a personal viewpoint, at that time in June 1974 the news left me both flabbergasted and quite angry. Hawkins was only 28 and had many good years left in him when the club saw fit to move him on.

It was a pitiful piece of business.

With Charlton now committed to a comeback, he took advantage of the opportunity provided by Jock Stein to turn out at Anfield in the Ron Yeats testimonial match...in the colours of Celtic! They were providing the opposition that evening, and by all accounts Charlton put on quite a show and even scored the opening goal in their 1-4 win.

Hay will be [illegible] "return" at Parkhead on August 12, a testimonial for Billy McNeill.

However, manager Jock Stein certainly didn't weaken his side by inviting Bobby Charlton to guest.

Charlton who is making a playing comeback next season with his club Preston North End, has lost none of his magnificent skills. He fitted superbly into the Celtic pattern, looking as though he had never played for anyone else.

Bobby Lennox thrived on the service, running the legs off the Liverpool defence on the left wing.

Ferocious

Charlton also proved that he has lost none of his ferocious shooting power, putting Celtic in front after 17 minutes with a devastating 18-yeard drive. Before half-time Vic Davidson and Lennox had shot Celts into a three-goal lead.

Harry Hood put Celtic 4-0 up eight minutes after the interval and it was not until

Credit: Glasgow Evening Times

As North End prepared for their now seemingly annual pre-season tour of Scotland, with matches at Raith Rovers and Dundee already arranged, the connection with Stein was maintained and Celtic threw down the welcome mat, hosting a celebration match for the North End manager which effectively doubled as another friendly. Charlton was afforded a guard of honour welcome in front of 11,000, and 'bhoyed' by this he scored the winning goal in an encouraging 1-2 North End win.

Credit: Daily Record

Bobby Charlton is applauded on to the pitch at Celtic Park

The new season of 1974/75 started well, with league wins against Plymouth Argyle, Walsall, Bury, Aldershot and Charlton Athletic, draws against Blackburn Rovers and Peterborough and a solitary – but close – defeat at Watford saw North End reach the summit of Division Three by the evening of 21st September.

With Charlton in fine form, and a crop of highly promising young players maturing under his guidance on the field, things looked rosy...but as *always* seemed the case with North End, they inexplicably descended into a barren patch – only gaining points from a bizarre home win over Bournemouth (who ended the game with nine men) and a draw at Hereford United, out of the next five games. Now placed fifth in the table, they needed to start moving in the right direction quickly.

CHAPTER 14

1974/75

BRIGHTON & HOVE ALBION V PRESTON NORTH END OCTOBER 19TH 1974

A lovely day at the seaside...

A few days training in Southport was Bobby Charlton's plan; his thoughts being that the team would benefit from a change of scenery before the long journey to Brighton. Little did he know just how much North End's liking for the sea air was to influence the result at the Goldstone Ground in a match that put North End back on track...for a little while at least.

Injuries were giving Charlton a headache for the second week running, but during the Southport training sessions, a now recovered Ray Treacy had demonstrated another string to his bow – as a midfield ball winner. More renowned for scoring goals, the Irish striker had been laid up since the summer following damage to his knee whilst in South America touring with the Republic of Ireland team, and had only recently returned to full training.

Charlton bit the bullet and decided to throw Treacy in at the deep end against Brighton. He would take over the number four shirt from Charlton, who would play a more forward role.

Brown, Spark, Burns, Treacy, Bird, Sadler, Lamb, Morley, Elwiss, Holden, Charlton. Sub: Baxter (S)

The line-up was certainly well balanced and not short on talent either, as they took to the pitch in the alternative kit of red and black striped shirts and white shorts.

It was Brighton who made all the early running, and they seemed to be attacking down Francis Burns' flank in particular. For all their early energy, Brighton never caused North End any real anxiety, and only a single shot by the lanky Ian Mellor actually tested John Brown in the North End goal.

North End collectively inhaled deeply – and the benefits of the sea air kicked in immediately! In the tenth minute, Mike Elwiss made a probing run down the inside left position, then centred the ball perfectly to meet Mel Holden's leap from the turf around seven yards out. Twisting in the air, his header beat goalkeeper Peter Grummitt before he could move, and the Lilywhites were one up! This was Holden's eighth goal of the season in just 13 appearances – continuing an excellent start to the season.

A renewed burst of energy from the hosts didn't result in much progress, with John Bird and David Sadler both on top of their game at the centre of North End's defence. Catching the eye though was the tough tackling Treacy, becoming the stumbling block of many a Brighton move. Not only the tackling; his distribution of the spoils was nigh on perfect too as he sent North End forward time and again.

North End began to own the game, and Alex Spark, relocated to right back in place of the injured John McMahon, was flying down the right flank at every opportunity to join in the attack. Preston looked like they had single-mindedly come to win this game and win it well.

A couple of free kicks were won around this point by North End, one in particular near the Brighton penalty area causing some interest. After Brighton lined up their wall, instead of a crashing Charlton shot, the crowd were treated to an extremely delicate high lob by the ex-England star that fell beyond the wall and was eventually just placed wide by Holden.

Ian Mellor barges into both Mel Holden and John Brown and concedes a free kick

It was from a Spark sortie down the right that North End eventually doubled their lead. After the Scot won a corner when Harry Wilson tackled him, Charlton trotted over to take the flag kick. Curling the ball in left footed towards the penalty spot, Holden leapt like a salmon to ping a header goalwards. He hit the post with that effort, but buried the rebound past Grummitt with another header just for good measure.

The half time whistle blew shortly afterwards, bringing a very satisfying first half to a close for North End. All the worries were the property of Brighton's manager, Peter Taylor as the teams refreshed themselves during the interval.

Brighton's response at the commencement of the second half was to come at North End all guns blazing, which would have been fine had they not kept losing the ball at the vital moments to a slicker North End outfit. After 10 minutes of huff and puff, the game resumed its first half shape, with North End controlling affairs.

Holden had a couple of great chances to complete his hat-trick around this time, a shot from the left of the area going just wide after an Elwiss pass had put him through, and a glancing header that was also placed just wide of the 'keepers left post.

Alex Spark watches as John Brown collects the ball at the feet of Ricky Marlowe

North End kept coming forward and just before the hour went three up. With his back to goal, Elwiss received a pass from midfield just inside the penalty area on the right from Alan Lamb. Immediately swivelling, the potent striker smashed an unforgiving shot past the hapless Grummitt, leaving him the task of collecting the ball from the back of his net for the third time.

The North End performance was causing unrest on the Brighton terraces, as the home fans let their thoughts be known as Brighton kicked off – again. The decibel level was immediately raised as from the restart, Brighton lost the ball and North End moved forward again operating a lovely passing movement as they went, the finishing shot from Holden passing just wide of the post.

Treacy, the root cause of Brighton's midfield impotence was having a blinder of a game. He was revelling in this new role but with the boos sounding out loud from the home fans, he was becoming the target of some rough treatment due to the frustration of his Brighton opposite, Billy McEwan.

At one point, McEwan appeared to kick Treacy while he was on the deck, but the referee shied away from sending him off – or even booking the former Blackpool player, choosing only to lecture instead. It made no difference whatsoever, as the Northender resumed his starring role after being dealt with by trainer Harry Hubbick.

Leisure and Football POST
Lancashire Evening Post

Guest Writer
MY SOCCER REVOLUTION
Page 2
By Norwich's JOHN BOND

BOBBY CHARLTON
THANKS PNE FANS
Page 3

Two-goal Mel tolls Brighton's knell

PNE HIT FOUR ON A SEASIDE SPREE!

PRESTON rediscovered their best form at Brighton today when they thrashed the South Coast team 4-0 to get back among the challengers for promotion to the Second Division.

The goals were scored by Mel Holden, with headers in the 10th and 44th minutes, by Mike Elwiss, who beat Brighton 'keeper Peter Grummitt with a superb shot after 58 minutes, and by Tony Morley in injury time, but all the North End ...

By NORMAN SHAKESHAFT

A mistake by Burns almost led to a Brighton equaliser but the North End defence survived and the game settled down.

Charlton had a shot from a free kick which was blocked by a Brighton wall of defenders while the home forwards also found it hard going ...

Just as the game went into injury time, Brighton won their first corner of the match. It came to nothing, but as if to rub salt into the wounds, Treacy went down the field and crossed the ball for Tony Morley to bag North End's fourth goal.

What a complete and utter annihilation this had been, and as the LEP Football Post reported, *'a goal spree.'* North End moved into fourth position, now two points behind leaders, Blackburn Rovers.

Sadly, this was another season that was to end in disappointment, not in relegation – but finishing a frustrating ninth, and during the latter part of the season seemingly as always just off the pace.

Transfer incomings, and indeed outgoings had been restricted to the sole arrival of Roy Tunks from Rotherham United. Better still, a promising pool of young gifted players had by now benefited from playing with and being coached by the legendary Charlton, and were ready to fly. Elwiss, Morley, Holden, Lamb, Gordon Coleman, Ricky Thomson, Mick Baxter, Gary Williams and Mark Lawrenson would probably have taken North End to the stars if there hadn't been a policy of 'sell first' at Deepdale in those days.

In fact, Charlton had hung up his boots for good long before the end of the season, his last game being at Port Vale on March 29th 1975. It's fair to say he had done his bit by then and the emerging talent needed occupying.

The campaign ended with North End finishing just seven points short of an immediate return to Division Two. Injuries were a legitimate excuse Charlton could cite for falling behind in the promotion race with McMahon, Lamb and Sadler all out for protracted periods of time. However, there was little reason why North End couldn't prosper in 1975/76 given a fair wind.

Such crystal ball gazing came to an abrupt halt early in the close season, when an out-of-the-blue £120,000 offer from Sunderland for the services of Mel Holden was readily accepted by the board, giving

Charlton his first reason to reach for the headache tablets. The board had subliminally sent Charlton a message.

When he was reported as saying that he had *'no idea how to fill the gap'* it rested uneasy with the North End supporters and rumours started suggesting another player 'fire sale' was on the way.

This was denied and Charlton issued an 'all is well' statement including the classic line that *'the directors are right behind me...'*

CHAPTER 15

CHARLTON, THE BOARD AND THE AFTERMATH

Nobody was prepared for the explosive news that broke on Thursday, August 21st 1975 following a North End Board meeting.

'Discussions took place upon a possible transfer deal involving John Bird in exchange for Alex Bruce plus £50,000. The manager informed the board that unless negotiations were broken off, he would resign his position. The board pointed out to the manager that the transfer deal would proceed and the accepted the managers resignation with regret.'

The national papers, radio and television all picked up on the story and gave it blanket coverage. Preston North End, Charlton, Bird – his captain – and the board were the talk of the whole football world ...who in the most sided with Charlton.

Unlike Alan Ball immediately before him, Charlton appears to have been unwilling to play the 'sell big, buy small' game that had brought such stress and frustration to whoever occupied the manager's chair at Deepdale. It was the manager that the fans would initially chant abuse at when it was all going wrong; taking the flak for decisions he had absolutely no control over.

The later editions of the LEP captured the gravity of the announcement

Lancashire
Evening Post
FINAL EDITION

THURSDAY, AUGUST 21, 1975

£100-worth of jewellery to be won

CHARLTON QUITS

Sensational end to transfer row

By NORMAN SHAKESHAFT

BOBBY CHARLTON today resigned as manager of Preston North End. His shock decision followed a disagreement with the board of directors over a proposed transfer deal.

"I am having to leave as a matter of principle," Charlton said following the board's decision to go ahead with what he described as an "unrealistic" transfer deal involving centre half John Bird, and Newcastle United.

"The directors insisted that for economic reasons they could not refuse money offered by Newcastle plus a player in exchange for John Bird but

NORTH END PLAYERS HIT OUT AT BOARD

The Preston North End players held a meeting at Deepdale this afternoon following the news of Charlton's resignation and issued a joint statement, criticising the board.

"We want to make it perfectly clear that we are very much against what has happened," they said.

"We feel the spirit has never been higher at Deepdale than in recent weeks.

"Now we will play against Port Vale on

LEP front page Thursday, August 21st 1975

DAILY EXPRESS Friday August 22 1975

Bobby Charlton quits on principle, then...

PRESTON REVOLT

SPORTS OPINION

Who's in charge—manager or board?

By Alan Thompson

PRESTON NORTH END players revolted against the club yesterday when they heard that manager Bobby Charlton had quit after a row with the directors.

Scottish Under-23 international midfield player Alex Spark handed in a written transfer request. Defender John McMahon, on the verge of joining Manchester United on loan, says he will not play for Preston at Port Vale tomorrow.

By John Roberts

Skipper John Bird, subject of the dispute that led to Charlton's resignation, said:—

"I am stunned and shocked and on behalf of the other players, as skipper, I can say that they are shocked, too."

'Sick'

Courtesy

Bobby Charlton turns his back on Preston North End

THE £10,000 GOALS CHASE

I'm not finished —Charlton

Francis facing a double problem

By Steve Curry

Beware of Hopalong the certified striker

ERIC MORECAMBE

ERIC MORECAMBE talking to NORMAN GILLER

Credit: Daily Express

Daily Express back page, August 22nd 1975

with the banner headline, **'CHARLTON QUITS – Sensational end to transfer row'**

Charlton was quoted as saying,

"I am having to leave as a matter of principle. The directors insisted that for economic reasons they could not refuse the money offered by Newcastle plus a player in exchange for John Bird, but I am not prepared to back the deal. The director's assessment of the value of Bird simply does not match mine and I will not have players at the club I do not want.

"As far as I'm concerned neither Alex Bruce nor Mick Burns could get a place in my team. If the directors are going to make decisions and just want somebody to carry them out they can get anybody to do that.*

"The directors think the deal is in the best interest of the club, but I don't. Basically that's what it's all about. I value John Bird much more highly than the directors do.

"I have worked hard for two years to get the players I want and don't see why I should have to run the club with players I don't want. I disagree with the deal, the valuations and everything.

"Everybody wants to put things on a financial footing, but how you get there is a matter of opinion. I have no desire to be the manager of a very wealthy non-league club."

"I had made my mind up beforehand what I would do if the directors decided to proceed with the negotiations with Newcastle – I would be leaving Deepdale as soon as I could settle my affairs."

**(Ex Blackpool winger Burns was offered as a possible alternative to Bruce by Newcastle United to North End)*

I never really understood that *'Bruce wouldn't get in my team'* statement from Charlton. In the previous season he had stated, as rumours strengthened of a £150,000 transfer bid from Sunderland for the Scot, *"I have no intention to sell, Alex is a vital player in our plans..."* There was more to this affair than met the eye.

What about the players? What effect had all this had on them? They were in deep shock at the happenings, held a meeting of their own, and issued the following statement.

"We want to make it perfectly clear that we are very much against what has happened. We feel that the spirit has never been higher at Deepdale than in recent weeks. We will now play against Port Vale on Saturday and give our best for the club if only for the sake of Bobby. We wish he was still with us and feel that a manager must be allowed to manage.

"We think the directors should concentrate on raising money for the club and leave the football to the professionals."

This aspect of the Charlton saga ballooned overnight, and the national papers the following day were quoting John McMahon as saying, *"I won't be playing for any Preston team on Saturday – that's how bad I feel about today."*

Apparently Charlton had arranged a trial at Manchester United for the full back, a move which the board had now thoughtlessly rescinded and trodden all over after the managers resignation. *"I don't want to kick another ball for this club,"* added a bitterly disappointed McMahon.

Meanwhile Nobby Stiles, whilst agreeing to take charge for the rest of the week was considering his own future at Deepdale. He was going to put his arm around McMahon and have a chat.

What an unholy mess.

In just two and half years, the board had seen off two decent managers – one by the sack, one by resignation. Both of those managers had shown the board the higher echelons of Division Two during their tenure, both desperately wanted the club to succeed. One had departed broken hearted that he wasn't allowed to continue the job, the other apparently no longer prepared to take part in boardroom shenanigans and witness his own hopes and ambitions – and those of the team – repeatedly curtailed.

Indeed it is very wise to be financially aware when running a football club, but it is not like any other business enterprise. It requires regular, sometimes large financial input and imaginative lateral thinking about how to raise funds – and sight must never be lost of the fact that without success in some shape or form on the football pitch, there is no point in existing at all!

Was it stretching the imagination too far to expect the board to ever think about approaching the council and opening negotiations with a view to buying the Deepdale ground from them in perhaps a series of instalments? Those painful outward transfers could have eventually paid for a tangible fixed asset over time which would have enabled the club to enjoy an overdraft in line with most other clubs and actually move forward on the pitch instead of being slammed into reverse every six months.

There was no such forward drive, ideas or investment at Deepdale. Board seats were occupied by the same people year in, year out who implemented the same old doctrine.

Charlton was initially funded when the board reformed in 1973, but once that been eaten up it was the usual return to default – a demand of attainment and success from the manager whilst the directors operated a policy of restriction and control in the background.

In fact during Charlton's tenure, the club had profited by £100,000 from transfer dealings; under Ball it was a massive £190,000, or £110,000...depending on who you think agreed to pay Manchester City for Neil Young and Dave Connor on the never-never. How much more could these managers have done?!

The eventual outcome of the board's ill conceived and suicidal financial policy would manifest itself early in the following decade as Preston

North End hurtled to the bottom of the professional game. It took the club to the brink of bankruptcy, as it eventually reached the bottom of the spiral of decline. Only then was the jolt big enough for some creative thinking to take place, resulting in Keith Leeming and Barney Campbell approaching the council with a view to laying a plastic pitch.

Gordon Lee, who was Newcastle United manager at the time of the Bird saga became North End manager early in the 1980's. His CV was impressive – Port Vale, Blackburn Rovers, Newcastle United, Everton – the one thing no one could doubt was his football experience. After being sacked by North End around the time the club's solvency was being openly questioned, he spoke for all those who had gone before him when he called the Preston manager's position, *"the hardest in football."*

Years later, Preston North End chairman at the time, Alan Jones said of Charlton's resignation, *"Bobby went over his 'point of principle' but significantly, he never returned to football management,"* implying that Jones didn't think Charlton was cut out for the job. A lot of fans agreed at the time – including myself – but when I read those words now, I wonder if it is any real surprise that he called time on football management after his final, awful Deepdale experience?

With Charlton gone, Stiles talked McMahon around and the team secured a draw at Port Vale. By the middle of the following week Stiles, still upset at Charlton's treatment, had resigned too and the board were in the process of meeting Harry Catterick with a view to offering him the position of 'General Manager' and Alan Kelly the post of 'Chief Coach.' Kelly scuppered that by refusing to take the job, saying it would be unfair to Catterick if he did so.

"I will stay on at Deepdale as reserve team coach for the time being; there have been too many comings and goings and I don't want to disrupt things anymore.

I will also look after the first team players until the new manager settles in properly because I don't want to let the club down."

Transfer talk concerning Bird went quiet for a week or so and from a personal point of view, I hoped we had heard the last of it.

John Bird outside the Lowthorpe Road players entrance amid all the confusion on August 21st 1975

What exactly was John Bird's take on all this? At the time it was only, *"I'm stunned and shocked"* but in 2015, Bird was interviewed by a reporter from the *Yorkshire Post*, who spoke to him about his journey through football and into the world of serious art.

Touching on the subject of the Charlton saga, Bird revealed that Lee had apparently already made a secret approach to the North End board for him and told him this after a chance meeting. Charlton however had been left out of the loop. Bird added, *"...so I approached Bobby the next day, and he said I know why you are here. You're staying at Preston – but if that lot sell you, I'm off."*

Bird was transferred and Alex Bruce was happy to return to the North End fold – with Newcastle United paying an extra £50,000 balance. Interestingly Bird also gave an insight into how his wages had grown since he had started out at Doncaster Rovers in 1971.

Modestly he starts, *"I was a steady defender* (he was very talented), *earning £20 a week plus £5 appearance money at Doncaster, £30 and £10 at Preston, and £1,200 a week at Newcastle."*

Even back in those days the top division was poles apart in terms of players wages!

Catterick moved into the Deepdale hot seat within the week. The board's position had obviously been made clear to him, as he stated in an interview for the LEP *"...buying and selling is the reality of football economics and it is essential to sell from time to time..."* which is true, but fails however to mention the randomness of the then Preston North End Board, who effectively pulled the rug from under whoever was manager!

Stiles was asked to reconsider his resignation and eventually returned to Deepdale as first team coach with Kelly retaining his reserve team duties.

The season of 1975/76 had begun well under Charlton. Two encouraging wins and his youthful team were looking set for big things after being bedded in during the previous season. Certainly the players had a good feeling as to what was around the corner, as their collective statement to the press upon hearing of Charlton's demise clearly indicated. Only time would tell if this optimism would translate into promotion back to Division Two.

CHAPTER 16

1975/76

PRESTON NORTH END V SHEFFIELD WEDNESDAY MARCH 30TH 1976

Not good enough...yet

As it happened, North End just weren't ready to progress into Division Two by the end of season 1975/76. The campaign was very stop-go as North End would often fail to capitalise on a few successive wins by frustratingly delivering a few successive defeats. This was reflected in the final analysis of their league position of eighth:–

Played 46, Won 19, Drawn 10, Lost 17, Goals for 62, Goals against 57, Points 48

Frustratingly, this left the team eight points short of Millwall in third place – the final promotion spot.

On the other hand, the younger players who had progressed through the ranks were beginning to bloom and were utilised well. Gary Williams, Mark Lawrenson, Stephen Doyle, and John Smith all became regulars during the season alongside the ever present Mike Elwiss who also bagged the title of leading goalscorer that season with 16 goals. His partnership with Alex Bruce (15 goals) was formidable; one of those heavenly occurrences that happens all too rarely at a football club. Together they were lethal and single minded in their search for goals, and certainly the most potent duo in the division.

There was no joy or indeed much needed income in the FA Cup either, as the Lilywhites exited heads bowed, at the second hurdle at non-league Scarborough.

Harry Catterick had been allowed to bring in Jimmy Brown from Aston Villa, (29 appearances) and Danny Cameron from Sheffield Wednesday (late in the season), for next to nothing.

At the December AGM however, despite the sale of John Bird earlier in the season the board announced that they were still losing £80,000 a year with home gates factored in at a level of 9,000. *"To go into the transfer market at the present time would be suicidal and irresponsible. It is a question of survival or bankruptcy and I hope you will support the board,"* pleaded Chairman Alan Jones.

Early in the New Year, the board, as so often in the past, struck again without warning. Tony Morley, the exceptional talent that by 1982 would be both a League Championship and European Cup winner with Aston Villa – due in no small part to his fantastic, marauding wing play – was airlifted out of Deepdale and dropped into Turf Moor for £100,000.

The board would see the absurdity of their commerce with Burnley manifest itself with even lower home crowds in the second half of the season, as the paying customers again voted with their feet. Lower crowds mean lower income – we all know the rest...

By mid-March 1976, North End were giving it one last go on the pitch, their fading hopes of a third place finish now usually discussed with the rider *"while it's still mathematically possible"* by the press.

On the penultimate day of the month, Sheffield Wednesday were due at Deepdale. They were in desperate straits themselves, bang in the middle of a frantic relegation fight. Their manager, Len Ashurst, promised they would be going to fight North End all the way for the points; those same points that North End needed themselves to keep their season alive.

It was a cool, dry evening as the teams took to the field in what turned out to be a crowd of just under 7,000.

Stood on the West Paddock towards the Kop end for this game, I was hoping beyond hope for a good win to keep the promotion hopes alive – regardless of the mathematics!

North End lined up with:-

Tunks, McMahon, Williams, Doyle, Sadler, Lawrenson, Brown, Coleman, Smith, Elwiss, Bruce. Sub: Spark

Frustratingly, North End seemed lethargic in the opening exchanges, and Wednesday were clearly the team on a mission. Mick Prendergast, the visitors' stalwart striker was twice served nicely when in front of the North End goal – once by Derek Bell, and once by the livewire Eric Potts – but contrived to fluff both opportunities.

With this warning siren registered by the home defence, the Lilywhites gradually asserted themselves and began to play the better football.

In the 21st minute North End went ahead when Mike Elwiss netted his 13th goal of the season, when a cross from the left from Jimmy Brown was contested by Wednesday goalkeeper, Peter Fox and John Smith a good 15 yards from Fox's goal line. The ball bounced towards goal, and under heavy challenge from centre half Dave Cusak, Elwiss managed to stretch out his right leg far enough to flick the ball past the giant defender and into the Kop net .

Doyle caught the eye, if only for the way he niggled the opposition – whoever North End were up against! He could play football, but the number of fouls he gave away was ridiculous! I often wondered if Nobby Stiles was fashioning Doyle's game on his own. These days I often wonder if Doyle is related to Ben Pearson! He certainly got in amongst it and more often than not came out on top.

A snap shot from Alex Bruce after a neat through pass by John McMahon was parried to safety by Fox, before a curling shot (or was it really a centre), from Brown skimmed the Wednesday crossbar.

Stephen Doyle gets in a header during an early North End attack against Sheffield Wednesday

Just before the interval, Eric Potts was cutting in from the right and heading menacingly towards Roy Tunks before the long legs of Mark Lawrenson slid alongside him and hooked the ball from under his feet. The defender then regained his own feet in one movement, steadied himself and passed the ball forward to appreciative applause from the crowd. Class.

The second half was in its infancy when the visitors sent North End back to square one with a neat equaliser by Derek Bell following good approach play from Prendergast and the lanky Roger Wylde.

North End soon got back on top and started to camp in the Wednesday half, passing the ball well and building pressure. It was John McMahon who pushed North End's noses in front however, when a corner from Brown was only partially cleared. The ball managed to travel 25 yards or so away from the goal line before the wholehearted full back treated the crowd to one of his trademark goals – the ball zooming into the net via a full swing of his right boot.

John McMahon scores North End's second goal with an unforgiving drive

That was in the 56th minute, by the hour North End had followed up and put clear water between themselves and the relegation candidates.

An Elwiss cross from the right after a fine run by the striker down the flank was knocked back intelligently by Smith directly into the path of Bruce who, as one had come to expect, drilled the ball home mercilessly.

Hard on the heels of that well worked success came a gift wrapped freebie courtesy of Potts to give North End their fourth goal, and Bruce his second in a quite remarkable opening 20 minutes to the second half.

The Wednesday players had already half turned to move up the field as Potts was in the act of executing a back pass to Fox – but Bruce hadn't – he was hovering around the advantage line waiting to see the outcome. Suddenly, like a golden eagle swooping on its prey, he was off and intercepted the under hit ball, side stepped the advancing and flailing

Fox, took the ball towards the goal and crashed it home past the desperate lunge of Peter Mullen with the home crowd's screams of anticipation turning to cheers of jubilation.

It was near the end of proceedings when Wednesday pulled a goal back, when Phil Henson headed home following a Gary Hull centre from the right to make the score look a little more respectable.

Catterick was very satisfied with the performance. *"We fully deserved our victory and there was a fine dressing room spirit that has taken time to produce.*

"All the lads played for one another and our youngsters showed they are beginning to learn the game. They also put in a tremendous amount of effort and played some fine football."

After rounding the Sheffield Wednesday 'keeper (centre), Alex Bruce steadies himself before slamming the ball into the net for North End's fourth goal

Typically in that season as the record books show, North End couldn't follow up this excellent win again, only managing a draw four days later at bottom of the table Colchester United, then going down by a single goal at Ninian Park to second placed Cardiff City. The season really was effectively now over, and the fans had to be content with the eighth place finish.

It was around this time that North End were notified that one of their prized fixed assets, the Willow Farm training facility, was to be the subject of a compulsory purchase order; this coming at the same time as the club were considering dispensing with another facility – the club's hostel for young players.

Just before the commencement of the new season, the board made a public statement about the clubs finances. The bottom line – and of most interest to the fans was the totally unrealistic statement – *'if attendances average 12,500 in the new season the board will not be looking to sell players.'*

Selling Bird and Morley had apparently saved the club £123,000 in losses over the season...but what if they had been kept? Would North End have garnered those extra nine points to achieve promotion?

Football at that time was on the cusp of becoming generally unpopular as a spectator sport. Crowd troubles, decrepit grounds and of course the ever increasing expense was about to herald over a decade of declining crowds, particularly outside of the top division. Indeed, only three times during the 1975/76 season had North End's home attendance broken through the 10,000 barrier, and the average for the season is logged at 7,072. It was highly unlikely therefore, that the board's target figure of 12,500 for 1976/77 would ever be accomplished.

Was this all a ploy for 'business' to continue as normal? It was totally unrealistic of the board to expect attendances to leap by over 56% while they continued to operate a policy of 'no investment, sell big, buy small.'

We had been warned.

CHAPTER 17

1976/77

PRESTON NORTH END V PETERBOROUGH UNITED OCTOBER 12TH 1976

The 'Posh' are pummelled...

In keeping with the previous season, transfer incomings were similarly restrained for the 1976/77 campaign. Additions to the North End squad amounted to two bargain basement players – experienced goalkeeper Alex Smith, as cover for Roy Tunks and Barrie Mitchell, a Scottish forward who had failed to agree terms with Tranmere Rovers during the close season.

The on-field performances of the club would be very similar to that of the previous season too. A slow start, followed by a long period of consistency without taking the division by storm, saw North End handily placed in fifth position in Division Three at the end of March – just three points behind leaders Mansfield Town.

April was fixture laden – eight matches within its 30 days with 16 crucial league points at stake. North End managed to glean just five at this most crucial part of the season, and despite 'getting back on the horse' with five points from six in the final three games in May, could only clamber back up the table to finish in sixth position.

The general feeling of the average North End fan such as myself, was that although promotion had been missed by six points, the season was one of general improvement. This was due in the main to an improved defensive record, but deference was also due to the brilliant forward partnership of Mike Elwiss and Alex Bruce who eventually plundered 45 league goals between them during the season out of a grand total of 64.

Whenever the annals of North End are read, this potent, dynamic and unrelenting duo will be rightly revered and surely seen as comparable to any other pair of renown that has graced the clubs long history.

Back in October of that season, North End were picking up the pace after a slow start. They entertained Peterborough United at Deepdale on Tuesday 12th, and produced their heaviest win for 10 long years.

North End skipper John McMahon failed a late fitness test on a hamstring injury so sat this game out. The North End team on this extremely wet autumn evening was:-

Tunks, Coleman, Williams, Burns, Sadler, Lawrenson, Doyle, Brown, Mitchell, Elwiss, Bruce. Sub: Smith (J)

The game began and North End soon penned the visitors back with positive forward movement. The ball was pinging across the surface assisted by the wet grass as the moves were built, and once or twice accidentally over hit into touch.

Despite dominating the early exchanges, it still came as a surprise when North End took the lead, or rather the manner of it did, after six minutes. Alex Bruce teed himself up for a shot at goal but seemingly mishit his drive, however Eric Steele the 'Posh' goalkeeper, contrived to make a complete hash of collecting the ball which somehow appeared to bobble through his legs and into the net!

The visitors pluckily came back with a fine response around the 15 minute mark, with a slick move that cut North End apart. Jon Nixon crossed the ball into the North End box from the left, and David Bradford cleverly flicked the ball backwards and across directly into the path of Ernie Moss, who took aim and fired past the diving Roy Tunks to equalise.

Within the next 10 minutes or so North End would regain the lead, the goal being scored by Barrie Mitchell. The former Aberdeen, Dunfermline and Tranmere striker made no mistake after he found himself in acres of space after being played in by the lively Bruce. After his shot hit the back of the net, neatly placed wide of Steele, he ran across to celebrate the goal with his fellow Scot.

Barrie Mitchell (left) and Alex Bruce celebrate North End's second goal

Minutes before half time, it was Bruce – once again in the thick of the action – who scored the third after a snap shot caught Peterborough centre back Chris Turner's rump and flew into the net, completely wrong footing the now thoroughly dismayed Steele. It had been a bad night for him so far!

Discussions at half time were limited as the rain had started again and I remember looking at the Town End asking myself, *'why oh why didn't you go in there?!'* from my West Paddock viewpoint. The weather had obviously affected the size of the crowd somewhat; Deepdale couldn't be described as anything else but 'sparsely populated.' In fact the crowd was officially registered at a very underwhelming 5,671 – way down on the board's expectations!

The second half commenced, John Smith had replaced hamstring casualty Mitchell, both sides were on all out attack...and the rain had stopped! It really was a great spectacle on such a miserable evening and the goals would keep on coming.

It was Noel Cantwell's men who were out of the blocks first. With Tunks beaten, Moss had a header cleared off the North End line by Jimmy Brown who stretched upwards and sideways to make the all-important contact, and a few minutes later Tunks pulled off a tremendous save when he tipped away a David Gregory 'screamer' for a corner.

After 65 minutes, North End effectively sealed the win when Bruce struck his hat trick goal and North End's fourth after neat interplay with strike partner Mike Elwiss. It was the latter whose forward thrust after receiving a through ball created the opportunity and Bruce made absolutely no mistake as he drilled the ball into the Town End net.

Chances from Francis Burns, Mark Lawrenson and Gordon Coleman were then spurned as North End threw the kitchen sink at a now bedraggled looking Peterborough team. Another goal was surely coming, and with 12 minutes left, it arrived when Elwiss scored direct from a free kick, when he skilfully eased the ball around the wall and beyond the reach of the demoralised Steele.

With just under 10 minutes left, there was still time for another couple of goals – North End grabbing the first, to take the score to 6-1. Gary Williams progressed forward and curled a centre into the box towards Smith and Bruce – with substitute Smith winning the contest, heading home into the bottom right corner.

The visitors, pummelled during the second half, pulled themselves up and scored the archetypal consolation goal following a move on the break. Bob Doyle ran forward from midfield with the ball as North End were caught up field; he centred it, finding team mate Jim Walker coming in from the left who duly headed past Tunks to make it 6-2.

John Smith (12) heads home North End's sixth goal

It was a tremendous win, and Harry Catterick was *'delighted'* with the performance. Chairman Alan Jones had declared on the eve of the match that, *"It was time for a big push to join the promotion contenders,"* and while North End's win certainly did that, was he more buoyed by the news in the LEP that scouts from Tottenham Hotspur, Liverpool, Leeds United, Everton, Coventry City and Birmingham City were becoming regular spectators in the stand wherever North End were playing?

At the December AGM, it was reported that the average home crowd was hovering below 8,000 – only two thirds of what the board considered the break-even point. The playing staff had been pared down to 20 plus six apprentices, and after a deepening rift, links with the Supporters Club' had been severed. The board policy remained 'survival.'

Following that austere message, a suggestion was made via the pages of the LEP by reporter Norman Shakeshaft urging the directors to double their personal guarantees to the bank.

During the close season the board gave their answer; there would be no new money going into the club – instead the board hung price tag labels around four of their outstanding players.

The PNE Board meeting minutes of 13th June 1977 record, *"After lengthy discussion it was agreed that the transfer of a player should be negotiated with minimum clear requirements being as follows: Lawrenson £100,000, Williams £45,000, Bruce £120,000, Elwiss £100,000."*

Brighton & Hove Albion wasted no time in relieving North End of Lawrenson *and* Williams; North End receiving £120,000 plus the experienced centre back Graham Cross and full back Harry Wilson in return.

Wherever would the North End board have been without the rich seam of youth to repeatedly pick at and plunder, selling on to other more ambitious clubs...and more to the point, wherever would the club have been have been by now if some of those players had been kept?

There was one more notable, indeed, significant piece of news during the close season. Nobby Stiles was to take over as manager. Reserve team coach Alan Kelly would be promoted to become his assistant, with Harry Catterick moving aside to take up a more general role within the club.

Following the stability of the previous decade, the directors had changed the North End manager on average every two and a half years in the Seventies. Stiles had done an excellent job at Deepdale to date in whatever position he had occupied.

Was he the man to finally drive the famous old club onwards and upwards?

Nobby the boss

MEET THE new bosses of Preston North End—big-smiling Nobby Stiles (right) and his assistant Alan Kelly.

Former England and Manchester United ace Stiles yesterday accepted the manager's job—two seasons after turning it down.

He steps up to take over from Harry Catterick who has been offered "an advisory position" at the same salary but has asked for a few days to think it over.

A delighted Stiles said: "I didn't feel ready for the post when Bobby Charlton quit two seasons ago. I was happy to become coach and learn under Harry Catterick. Both Alan and I owe him a lot."

Stiles, who believes Catterick will stay with the club added: "Betwetn the three of us a lot of building has been done over the past two years. I think the results of that effort will begin to show in the coming season."

Preston chairman Alan Jones said the changes were in the best interests of the club.

Credit: Daily Mirror

July 22nd 1977, and the Stiles/Kelly partnership is launched…

CHAPTER 18

1977/78

PRESTON NORTH END V LINCOLN CITY APRIL 15TH 1978

North End star in TV goal fest

The season of 1977/78 was, and always will be, seen as a great triumph for the North End management team of Nobby Stiles and Alan Kelly.

In true North End tradition, the team – who had performed consistently well over the campaign – contrived to all but hand their promotion spot over to Peterborough at the very last hurdle, but in a must-win, nail-biting final fixture at Wrexham the 'Posh' could only manage a goalless draw and finished behind North End – and under the promotion line – on goal difference.

There had been some splendid performances during the season, both individually and collectively. The team was the classic blend for success; lots of eager but skilled youth bolstered by older heads in key areas.

Alex Bruce and Mike Elwiss shone like beacons up front, scoring 27 and 12 league goals respectively, thus taking their combined three season league tally whilst in partnership together to an astonishing 114. Young centre back Mick Baxter caught the eye playing alongside Graham Cross and in front of Roy Tunks, while the arrival in late September of Sean Haselgrave from Nottingham Forest allowed Stiles to bolster the midfield with a combination of experience and ability.

The Lilywhites seemed to have timed their run to perfection; at the end of March they stood second in the Division Three table, a position which they still held before they entertained 15th placed Lincoln City at Deepdale on April 15th.

This game was the first of the last five, part of a run-in that saw three games away from home. A good win was needed to cement North End into that second position until midweek at least, when they had to travel to Hillsborough to face Sheffield Wednesday.

The expectation was such that a decent crowd of 11,208 clicked through the turnstiles and even Granada TV were present, recording the match for Sunday afternoon transmission. There was a general apprehension whenever this occurred – with both players and fans – as North End never seemed to perform well in front of the cameras.

It was a cool but sunny spring day as the 'lads' ran out, North End lining up with:-

Tunks, McMahon, Cameron, Burns, Baxter, Cross, Coleman, Haselgrave, Robinson, Elwiss, Bruce. Substitute: Doyle.

Lincoln kicked off towards the Town End, and made some progress down the left. However, after a throw by Phil Hubbard that saw the ball won keenly in centre field by Francis Burns, trouble for the Imps was brewing.

Burns looked up, saw Danny Cameron running forward down the left wing and carved out a wonderful pass to enable him to progress forward. This he did, moving infield and eventually passing further forward to Alex Bruce as the striker entered the box from the left. Progress was halted as centre half Clive Wiggington thrust out a boot, conceding a corner.

Sean Haselgrave took the corner and sent it wide but the unmarked Mick Baxter was always underneath it and the ball ballooned high off his head to be headed clear of the box but only as far as John McMahon, 35 yards from goal. Twisting to the left, he created enough room to launch a cross completely unchallenged. The ball floated to the six yard line, where Wiggington, under challenge from the leaping Elwiss, could only head the ball across the face of goal where Mick Robinson leapt high to head past the rooted Lincoln 'keeper, Peter Grotier for his second goal in league football.

North End one up after three minutes, and it wasn't to stop there. After a couple of worthy moves had been played out – one for each side – Wiggington shooting wide of the North End goal and Burns shooting too high after neat work from Haselgrave, North End added another goal after 15 minutes.

In front of the West Paddock, Haselgrave threw the ball into Elwiss's path on the left wing. Running at the defenders, he managed to wrap his foot around the ball to deliver a wonderful cross to the near post, where right back Phil Neale was waiting to head the ball clear of danger and into the Kop.

Haselgrave curled the ball in from the flag kick and in what looked to be a set move; Robinson rushed forward and diving, glanced the ball into the goalmouth enabling Elwiss to shoot for goal from about four yards out. His initial shot was blocked by Neale and so was his follow up, the ball then rolled out in the direction of Baxter, all of seven yards out who drove a high, merciless shot in to the roof of the net.

The delighted North Enders mobbed the tall centre back as he made his way back down the pitch to take up his default position. North End were on fire, and the television bogey was finally about to be laid to rest.

After Neale (degree in Russian, century for Worcester against the West

Indians in 1976), had aimed hopefully at the North End goal, the ball was hooked forward by Cameron and eventually found its way to Robinson. His looped header from the edge of the box fell between a triangle of goalkeeper and defenders, as the ever alert Elwiss made a dash across the box for the loose ball. Elwiss won the race with Grotier, the ball somehow bouncing behind them both and into the path of Bruce just six yards out with a solitary defender on the goal line.

There was no hesitation.

Alex Bruce raises a clenched fist of solidarity towards the home fans after scoring

To loud cheers of delight, the net bulged as the ball was lashed in. From the Lincoln point of view the ball couldn't have fallen to anybody worse; Bruce was ruthless in front of goal, and as he was mobbed by his teammates the Lincoln defensive inquest began.

Despite the shellshock of going three down by the 25th minute, Lincoln stuck to their task and steadied their rocking ship. Their attack was led by a young Mick Harford, and he impressed more than once with his heading ability.

Elwiss was prominent for North End and had a roving type of role very similar to that of Paul Merson at Arsenal a decade later. He was frequently on the left side, running at and beating defenders before cutting in towards goal giving him the option of a shot or a pass. It was exciting and a pleasure to watch for yours truly, and one such move as the interval approached nearly resulted in a fourth North End goal.

Gordon Coleman passed the ball across the centre of the pitch to Elwiss. He controlled the ball and ran at right back Brendan Guest, taking the ball forward around 20 yards before cutting in and crossing the ball towards the back of the area. It found Coleman who headed forward into the path of Robinson whose shot on the turn agonisingly bobbled across the front of goal and into touch.

It took North End just 10 minutes of the second half to add a fourth goal, and again it was created by superb piece of play down the left by Elwiss. He controlled the ball from a throw-in by Haselgrave close to the left touchline.

With a quick lowering of the shoulder, defender Terry Cooper (no, not that Terry Cooper) was turned in an instant, and a superb left footed cross was punched in that was met by Robinson seven yards out. His header seemed destined for the bottom right corner, but at full stretch, Grotier only managed to palm the ball out as far as the onrushing Coleman who gleefully crashed the ball home from an oblique angle.

Preston continued to have most of the ball, but the visitors occasionally sprung into life and created an opportunity. Phil Hubbard lost control of the ball just outside the North End box, but it fell into the domain of Alan Harding whose rasping drive was turned away for a corner via the fingertips of Tunks, diving to this left.

On another occasion a Peter Graham cross towards the back of the area found the leaping Hubbard whose header was cleared off the line by

Graham Cross under pressure from Harford.

At the other end, Elwiss continued to torment the Lincoln left hand side, always seeming to have that extra yard and a half to create the opportunity. A great cross found Robinson but his header was saved by Grotier.

Baxter put Bruce through with a neat pass but his attempt was blocked by Grotier, narrowing the angle. Cameron then went close with a speculative shot, the ball fizzing past Grotier's left post. Just before the final whistle, the tireless Coleman hooked the ball just over the bar in what had looked like a lost cause as it bounced towards the byline.

Leisure and Football POST

Lancashire Evening Post

No. 28,328 SATURDAY APRIL 15 1978 8p

CAN LIVE THE EUR

Page

PNE HIT FOUR IN PROMOTION DRIVE

PRESTON maintained their strong challenge for promotion to Division Two when they beat Lincoln City 4-0 at Deepdale today in front of a crowd of 11,208.

North End had scored only two goals in their previous five League games, but they ended their 'famine' in an impressive first half display.

By NORMAN SHAKESHAFT

Mick Robinson, Mick Baxter and Alex Bruce had netted in this period and Gordon Coleman had clinched the result 10 minutes after the interval.

Ian St John, the 'Kick Off Match' pundit back then, gave the home crowd a bit of a blast when asked by commentator Gerald Sinsdadt for his opinion of the game. He was struck by there being, *"...only 11,000 people present compared to when I played in matches here in the past and they never really got behind their team. It seems like the players here have to do their thing before the fans react, rather than the other way about.*

"It is important that the crowd get behind the players at all times, especially going for promotion. They need this extra push from the crowd. It astounded me when I was sat in the stands hearing the level of criticism directed at the players – players who I thought played very well, but as soon as they made a mistake criticism was heaped on them. This doesn't help the team at all so I hope the Preston people get behind the players so they don't have to do it all alone."

Perhaps if 'Saint' had experienced a decade like those fans had, he would perhaps have understood the situation a little better!

A midweek trip to play Sheffield Wednesday was up next, and Preston underperformed, going down by the only goal. This lapse was critical; both Cambridge United and Peterborough closed the gap on North End and suddenly it was three teams chasing the two remaining promotion spots, discounting Wrexham who were already champions elect. Second and third placed North End and Cambridge United were now separated only by goal difference, both having 53 points. Peterborough in fourth place now held the advantage. Despite having only 52 points, crucially they had a game in hand.

North End *had* to win at Fratton Park against Portsmouth in their next outing, with now just three games remaining. No messing.

Team	Pl	W	D	L	F	A	GD	Pts
Wrexham	41	22	13	6	69	40	29	57
Preston North End	43	19	15	9	58	34	24	53
Cambridge United	43	21	11	11	69	50	19	53
Peterborough United	42	19	14	9	40	26	14	52

CHAPTER 19

1977/78

PORTSMOUTH V PRESTON NORTH END
APRIL 22ND 1978

Pompey resistance finally eroded

With Nobby Stiles stating that he *'wasn't flapping'* in a pre-match interview, the North End manager further demonstrated his confidence by naming an unchanged team for the fifth successive game:-

Tunks, McMahon, Cameron, Burns, Baxter, Cross, Coleman, Haselgrave, Robinson, Elwiss, Bruce. Substitute: Doyle

Both teams notched a corner apiece within the first few minutes, and indeed both were safely gathered by the respective goalkeepers. North End looked bright enough in an open first 15 minutes, while Portsmouth were looking to redeem themselves somewhat with their fans by beating a promotion favourite, having already falling through the division's trap door.

The North End defensive sirens were sounded when Steve Foster put in a header that required Graham Cross to clear off the North End line with Roy Tunks beaten.

At the other end, half chances fell for Alex Bruce and Mike Elwiss before John McMahon concluded another North End raid by shooting over the bar. Francis Burns then fired in a screamer from all of 30 yards that hit Steve Middleton the Pompey goalkeeper, before bouncing away to safety.

Michael Robinson challenging the Portsmouth 'keeper during a first half attack

As the game drew close to half time, there had been plenty of incident but not enough quality on display from North End to grab that vital opening goal.

It was obvious within a few minutes of the second stanza starting that North End had been instructed to 'up the ante' in this crucial game.

A long of goal attempts started to amass on North End's credit sheet, with close calls from Gordon Coleman whose 'goal' was disallowed, Mick Robinson who had a point-blank shot blocked by Middleton and Burns who shot over the bar – all in the space of 10 minutes.

Bruce then shot wide from a McMahon pass and then a free kick from the North End right back saw Middleton called into action yet again to tip Mick Baxter's header over the bar. Sean Haselgrave tried his luck, weaving his way through the Pompey lines only to see Middleton block his shot, and then Elwiss just failed to connect with a Danny Cameron pass that would have surely opened the scoring.

Alex Bruce fires in yet another shot during a spell of North End pressure

Time was ebbing way and frustration mounting for Preston as they drove forward again for another salvo at the home defences. McMahon, picking up the ball near the halfway line, moved forward and passed the ball to Elwiss. After making a few yards progress, he crossed the ball and found an unmarked Bruce available to bury a header into the back of the net. Finally!

Alex Bruce heads home the opening goal for North End

There was less than 10 minutes of time remaining and thankfully North End chose not to rest on their laurels and, after full back David Pullar had seen his shot saved by Tunks, the Lilywhites went straight upfield and helped themselves to another goal.

It was Robinson who squared the ball neatly across the box to Elwiss, some 15 yards out from goal and under pressure from the approaching full back Billy Wilson. As a result he wasted no time in driving his shot past the advancing Middleton to seal the win for North End.

Mike Elwiss drives home North End's second

Team	Pl	W	D	L	F	A	GD	Pts
Wrexham	42	23	13	6	76	41	35	59
Preston North End	44	20	15	9	60	34	26	55
Cambridge United	44	21	12	11	69	50	19	54
Peterborough United	43	20	14	9	41	26	15	54

It was yet another North End game that ended sporting the names of Bruce and Elwiss in the 'goals scored' column and with the points secured. The next task was to travel to Millmoor and face Rotherham United, a team in the lower reaches of the division. If North End kept winning, they could not be denied promotion. Two games remaining – it didn't go to plan!

CHAPTER 20

1977/78

PRESTON NORTH END V SHREWSBURY TOWN
APRIL 29TH 1978

Failing to tame 'The Shrews'

Perhaps 'not going to plan' was the understatement of 1978 for North End. It wasn't as though they turned up and put in an awful performance – far from it – the right tactics were employed throughout, but Rotherham, yes lowly Rotherham, played like men possessed and so determined were they to edge clear of any looming relegation worries, won the match by 2-1.

The failure of Graham Cross to unaccountably deal with a through ball was the catalyst that started North End's demise. From that mistake the Millers went ahead, totally against the run of bombardment their goalkeeper had received until that moment.

The game changed, as the home team suddenly believed that they could win no matter what the Lilywhites threw at them. Countless times there were scrambles and near misses at the Rotherham end before – yes, you've guessed it – they went 2-0 ahead.

Around 10 minutes from the end, Alex Bruce halved the deficit, and although North End piled on the pressure, deep down everybody knew how this was going to finish.

Sadly, this crucial defeat hides the fact that Mike Elwiss put in the performance of his life for the club that night. Strong and creative throughout, he was unbelievably denied on several occasions by some invisible force field that ringed the Millers' goalmouth.

The journey home from South Yorkshire was a long one that night for the many North End fans. Head scratching, imaginary permutations of the final Division Three table, and a sick realisation that North End's hopes were completely out of their hands now made for a subdued drive home. The league table after all the midweek games is below.

Manager Nobby Stiles put a positive spin on things.

"The defeat was a big blow and the players were very dejected after the game. They all worked very hard and never gave up until the final whistle. Rotherham played very well but so did we and I can't praise our lads enough for the effort they put in.

"However, we are now focused on Shrewsbury Town's visit to Deepdale on Saturday. The pressure is very much on Peterborough and Cambridge too, especially Peterborough who have two difficult away fixtures at Chester and Wrexham. If we can get the two points on Saturday we are still in with a good chance of promotion."

Team	Pl	W	D	L	F	A	GD	Pts
Wrexham	43	23	13	7	76	42	34	59
Cambridge United	45	22	12	11	70	50	20	56
Preston North End	45	20	15	10	61	36	25	55
Peterborough United	44	20	15	9	44	29	15	55

With just one game remaining and the weekend drawing ever closer, the tension rose...for everybody! Shrewsbury manager Richie Barker fanned those flames of anxiety when he pronounced on the eve of the game that it would give him, *"sadistic pleasure to prevent Preston's promotion,"* a view that Stiles understood fully. He expected *"nothing less,"* and assured the faithful that North End, *"will be going flat out for victory."*

A massive (for the era) 16,078 souls entered Deepdale on Saturday, April 29th 1978; the vast majority of them hoping beyond hope for a North End win. It had been a fantastic season despite the recent disappointments and North End's entrance to the arena was greeted by huge cheers and applause.

The conditions were mild and fine, the pitch surface looked ideal. Stiles named an unchanged team for the seventh consecutive game, while Barker was able to name the same Shrewsbury team for the sixth time in succession. They were obviously a settled outfit and had picked up 11 points out of a possible 14 in their last seven games.

North End lined up:-

Tunks, McMahon, Cameron, Burns, Baxter, Cross, Coleman, Haselgrave, Robinson, Elwiss, Bruce. Substitute: Doyle

I wonder how many of those fans replaying the match in their minds on the road back from Rotherham would have guessed the start North End would make in this final match; a game that just *had* to be won, built on the blood, sweat and tears of 45 previous games over the past eight months?

They were 0-1 down in the first minute!

An early innocuous foul conceded on the right flank mushroomed into an absolute nightmare as John King launched the ball into the North End box and striker Ian Atkins met it perfectly to head past Roy Tunks, immediately silencing the large home crowd. Joyfully expectant just a few seconds before, the North End fans were now staring at each other in silent bewilderment.

North End kicked off for a second time towards the Town End, now with a one goal handicap against their name.

Shaken into action, North End got to work. Four corners in succession promised much but brought no reward, and this spell of pressure was ended with Elwiss shooting narrowly wide. It was the visitors turn next with two quick-fire raids on the North End goal, Steve Biggins drilling his shot wide of the left post, and another Atkins header once again on target was this time foiled by Tunks.

This was brewing up into a good game, as North End came roaring back when neat interplay left Gordon Coleman in a position to launch a 25 yard drive that just went over the crossbar.

Atkins was posing a real threat down the middle, and it took a brave dive at the big strikers' feet at the critical moment by Tunks to deny him what looked from the West Paddock at least, a nailed on goal.

After Michael Robinson had won a corner on the right for North End after a good run, there was an almighty scramble in the visitor's goalmouth before the ball was finally – and thankfully for Shrewsbury – hoofed away.

A free kick was awarded to North End in the 38th minute, just outside the penalty area on the right hand side. Elwiss strode forward, and off a short run up lashed the ball through the visitor's wall leaving ex-Manchester City goalkeeper Ken Mulhearn with no chance between the Shrewsbury sticks. Mulhearn, having expected the wall to stand firm was left statuesque as the ball found the back of the net via the post.

This was Elwiss's 17th goal of the season in all competitions and nobody could say it wasn't deserved. The goal had the effect of lifting the home crowd again and giving them hope...for all of four minutes! That's how long it took Shrewsbury to regain the lead and reduce the home crowd to head-shaking wrecks again!

Francis Burns was in the process of passing the ball back to Tunks when Jack Keay decided there was an opportunity presenting itself. He managed to nip in between the Preston pair and get an outstretched foot to the ball, prodding it past Tunks.

There was enough time left in the half for North End to build a move that culminated in Robinson striking a rasping drive that Mulhearn finger-tipped away to safety. Despite this positive note, the team trudged off at half time no doubt wondering which one of them had run over a black cat. The harder they tried, the worse their luck seemed to get!

Everybody's eyes diverted when the two blokes who operated their respective half time scoreboards dashed out of the tunnel. All eyes were on letters 'B' and 'D' which represented Cambridge United v Exeter City and Chester v Peterborough United. Just before the players trotted on to the pitch for the second half, out hurried the two gentlemen in question.

Cambridge 0 Exeter 0, and wait for it...Chester 1 Peterborough 1. All still up in the air then, but North End had to win!

The second half commenced and North End went for it full throttle. Mick Baxter set the tone with a header that just flashed wide of the post, followed by a litany of close calls for the Shrewsbury defence. Elwiss played Alex Bruce in but his shot was inches wide, he then had a header well saved by Mulhearn, Robinson caned in a powerful shot that was blocked and after weaving past a couple of tackles and Sean Haselgrave placed a shot nearer to the cameramen than the inside of the post.

You couldn't take your eyes off this game for a moment as completely against the run of play Biggins almost made it 1-3, but headed wide following a swift counter attack.

The hour passed, and now North End had just 30 minutes to salvage something – anything – from this season. Shrewsbury were no fools and despite being under the cosh never panicked. They were absorbing the pressure and sticking to their counter attack plans. Stiles had to do something, and on 65 minutes replaced Robinson with Stephen Doyle. This released Coleman to assist the front line and enabled Doyle to add grit to the midfield.

Time was marching on and that sick feeling in the pit of the stomach was starting to become apparent in the North End faithful who nevertheless continued to urge their team on blindly from the terraces.

Elwiss powered down the left, centred and saw Coleman launch himself at the ball, but the header went just wide. In fact, the switch seemed to be working as Coleman was finding space and involving himself in a string of moves.

A foul by Keay led to a free kick on the left, which found its way to Coleman within shooting distance. The midfielder's shot was struck beautifully and homed in on Mulhearn's goal like a missile. Within milliseconds it hit the bar and bounced to safety, producing cries of disbelief from the home fans.

Desperation was setting in and with the defenders now joining in the attack whenever practical, North End were certainly not going to die wondering. Finally, in the 82nd minute North End were rewarded with an equaliser, just and overdue reward for their sustained all-out attack.

A cross from the right was neatly headed on by Baxter across to Bruce, who made good ground to head home his 30th goal of the season.

North End then threw everything at the Shrewsbury goal but despite close calls via the boots of Coleman and Baxter, the game ended 2-2.

While the younger elements of the crowd produced the now traditional end of season pitch invasion, I made a desperate dash to my car and get the radio on for the full time scores. Cambridge had won by 2-1 and were promoted. Chester had unbelievably beaten Peterborough 4-3, which meant North End were still alive albeit 50/50, in the promotion race.

The table on the evening of April 29th was thus:-

Team	Pl	W	D	L	F	A	GD	Pts
Wrexham	44	23	14	7	77	43	34	60
Cambridge United	46	23	12	11	72	51	21	58
Preston North End	46	20	16	10	63	38	25	56
Peterborough United	45	20	15	10	47	33	14	55

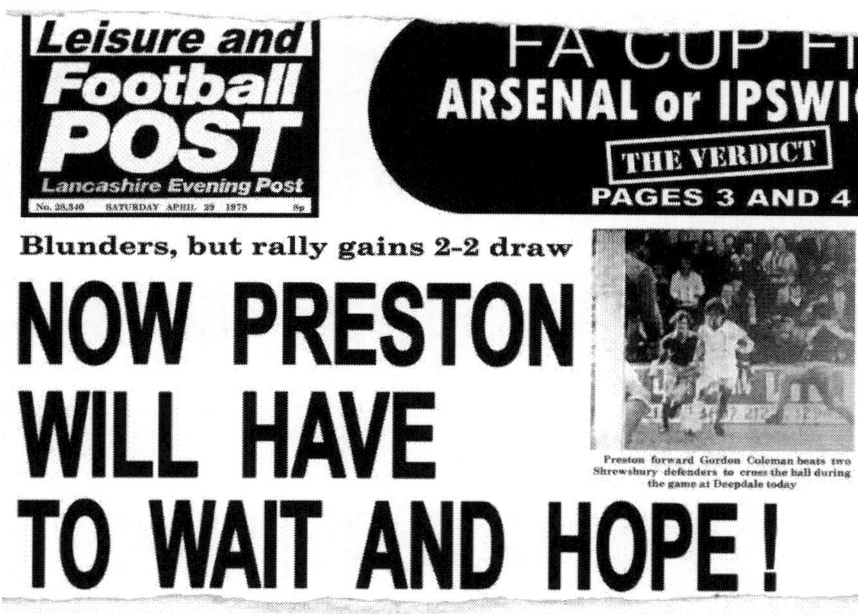
Leisure and Football POST
Lancashire Evening Post
No. 28,340 SATURDAY APRIL 29 1978 8p

FA CUP FI
ARSENAL or IPSWI
THE VERDICT
PAGES 3 AND 4

Blunders, but rally gains 2-2 draw

NOW PRESTON WILL HAVE TO WAIT AND HOPE !

Preston forward Gordon Coleman beats two Shrewsbury defenders to cross the ball during the game at Deepdale today

All this meant that with Peterborough failing to gather anything at Chester, they had to win their last game of the season as a draw would be insufficient due to their goal difference being inferior to North End's.

Peterborough's last game of the season? Why, it was away at top of the table Wrexham, and due to be played on Monday, 1st May – a brand new bank holiday!

There was an estimated 20,000 crowd at The Racecourse, amongst them Nobby Stiles, Alan Kelly, Francis Burns, chief scout Jimmie Scott, a few North End directors, and a whole swathe of North End fans.

Wrexham received the championship trophy before kick-off and managed to summon up enough strength to stem a strong Peterborough tide of attacks and near misses, their legendary goalkeeper Dai Davies producing a starring role in a goalless encounter.

The story goes that at half time, Stiles' cup was rocking in its saucer so nervous was he, but I'm not so sure. He had displayed sound common sense throughout North End's late season hiatus and had been in the game long enough to cope with a situation such as this. However, Jimmie Scott did admit it was *'a nerve wracking time.'*

Francis Burns had a troubled conscience. Here was a seasoned professional, who had enjoyed the Manchester United glory days at all levels and played alongside several greats of the game. A little bit of North End must have seeped into his blood though over the previous few years as he revealed he had *"suffered the worst weekend of his entire career,"* after being partly responsible for one of the Shrewsbury goals on the previous Saturday. He added that he was *"overwhelmed"* to arrive at Wrexham to find hundreds of North End fans already there ready to cheer on the home team.

The 'promise' of some cash for new players was immediately made by PNE Chairman Alan Jones, and a rumour instantly started that Ian Callaghan of Liverpool may be one of the targets. Stiles always played this link down however, insisting that the player could earn double any Preston salary by staying at Liverpool. In the end Callaghan opted to join up with ex Liverpool teammate, John Toshack at Swansea.

Wrexham went on to lose their last fixture 2-1 away to Sheffield

Wednesday, leaving the final table thus:-

Team	Pl	W	D	L	F	A	GD	Pts
Wrexham	46	23	15	8	78	45	33	61
Cambridge United	46	23	12	11	72	51	21	58
Preston North End	46	20	16	10	63	38	25	56
Peterborough United	46	20	16	10	47	33	14	56

The Scout: 30—1 TREBLE

DAILY EXPRESS

THE VOICE OF BRITAIN

Tuesday May 2 1978

NOBBY DAZZLER!

A great day as manager Stiles leads Proud Preston to promotion

By Bill Elliott

SOCCER great Nobby Stiles led Preston North End back into the Second Division the hard way yesterday.

The former Manchester United and England player did it while sitting in the stands at Wrexham.

End of the agony: See Back Page

DRAINED

Nobby Stiles celebrating at home with his greatest fans, sons John, 14, Peter, 12, and Robert, 9

Credit: Daily Express

OUT OF THE WILDERNESS!

Wrexham give Preston a helping hand into the Second division

By NORMAN SHAKESHAFT

PRESTON NORTH END are back in Division Two after four seasons in the Football League wilderness of the Third Division!

Promotion was assured at the Racecourse Ground yesterday when Peterborough failed to beat Wrexham, the new champions of Division Three.

A goalless draw in that game means that third-placed Preston go up on goal difference with a total of 56 points from 46 League fixtures, along with Wrexham, who clinched promotion more than a week ago, and second-placed Cambridge, who beat Exeter to make sure of going up on Saturday.

[illegible]

● RIGHT: Celebration ... at [illegible]! Preston fans invade the pitch after the draw with Shrewsbury on Saturday.

Cally: No decision

NEW players are likely to be signed by Preston North End before next season's campaign back in Division Two.

This was confirmed by both chairman Alan Jones and manager Nobby Stiles today after a board meeting at Deepdale last night.

But suggestions that Preston are ready to sign Liverpool's former England international midfield man Ian Callaghan are premature (writes NORMAN SHAKESHAFT).

IAN CALLAGHAN

It's finally over! North End are confirmed as finishing in third position on 'goal difference' after Peterborough fail to win their last outing at Wrexham

YESTERDAY'S FOOTBALL

Posh 'killed' by great Dai

By DAVID MOORE: Wrexham 0, Peterborough 0

FOUR stunning saves by Dai Davies deprived brave Peterborough of a Second Division place yesterday.

The Wrexham keeper's performance was watched by Nobby Stiles, manager of the Preston team who go up instead on goal difference.

Posh manager John Barnwell said: "We did enough to win. It was just our bad luck to encounter Davies at the height of his form.

Credit: Daily Mirror

CHAPTER 21

BRUCE & ELWISS – THE BEST NORTH END STRIKEFORCE OF MODERN TIMES?

At this juncture, it is worth noting the performance, quality and indeed distinction of the formidable North End attacking partnership of Alex Bruce and Mike Elwiss.

On statistics alone they were the best pairing since Alex Dawson and Brian Godfrey in the three-season period between 1963/64 and 1965/66. In that time, the Sixties duo racked up 131 goals in all competitions for the Lilywhites. Using the same yardstick, remarkably between 1975/76 and 1977/78 Bruce and Elwiss found the net 126 times – just five goals less.

Everybody knows and understands the argument that you cannot compare eras as so many of the *'terms and conditions'* are obviously different; the plain fact is you just have to accept the figures on the piece of paper and what you have witnessed with your own eyes.

I only saw the latter part of the Dawson/Godfrey combination due to my age, but remembered enough to see their qualities re-incarnate themselves just over a decade later in Bruce and Elwiss.

Although their physiques were quite different, both Dawson and Bruce had a remarkably similar working method – namely receive the ball, line up the crosshairs on the target and strike.

It served them well.

Dawson blasted in 80 goals in those three seasons in the Sixites, while Bruce hammered home 71 goals in the mid Seventies. Yes, of course they both contributed to the team in other ways, but not quite as much as their partners. They were single-mindedly focused on scoring.

Godfrey and Elwiss were more creative, possessing a more rounded game. Besides having the skill to score wonderful goals, they were also able to frequently unlock defences with golden touches of play. Their goal tally over their respective three seasons is very similar too – Godfrey 50 goals, Elwiss 55.

The telepathy, sixth sense – whatever you wish to call it, that transmits between such a pair is what makes their work unique and such an absolute joy for the fan to watch.

It's quite ironic that Elwiss arrived at Deepdale in March 1974 with cash raised from the transfer of Alex Bruce to Newcastle United just over a month previously. It may never have happened at all if Liverpool hadn't pulled out of signing Elwiss just a few months previously.

"I was about to sign for Liverpool a few months before I came to Preston, but the deal fell through. It was all about money; money between the clubs. Doncaster kept putting the price up and Liverpool started to say 'no.'

"Preston then came in and I was only too happy to come here. It was a good move and I really had a good time at Deepdale."

Bruce of course returned in August 1975, manager Bobby Charlton had departed and the terrorising of defences began as the pair hitched up.

"Alex and I were a good foil for each other and I served everything up on a plate for him whenever I could. We just complimented each other and

it was uncanny at times. Our blend was just right, which is rare in football."

Bruce, who I first saw in the North End reserve team, was a natural. Even then, he demonstrated not an ounce of fear when a chance fell to him, a trait that thankfully wasn't ever lost or coached out of him. He was merciless.

"Playing football with Mike Elwiss was a dream, and it felt like all my birthday's had come at once. In all those games I played with Mike I never saw his head drop once. He was as brave as a lion and a fantastic all-round footballer.

"It was very instinctive. Sometimes I would just stand on the edge of the six yard box and Mike would deliver. We were both in our prime, and there was a spell when I felt nothing could go wrong. It was like walking on water and Mike was the best striking partner I ever played with."

Personally, I am so pleased that I saw Bruce and Elwiss in their pomp. Elwiss showing the ball to the full back, taking him on, and then cutting inside ready to launch the killer cross to Bruce, waiting with striving determination to get on the end of it.

Manager Nobby Stiles saw the potential and knew exactly what he was doing when he gave them both 'free roles' in the team. Stiles nominated Elwiss to be his captain, his dynamic approach to matters on the pitch playing no small part in North End's appearance on the honours board in early May 1978.

"They were incredibly happy and enjoyable times at Preston. I say that from the heart because the whole experience was special.

"Those fantastic fans were superb to me and it was a truly memorable time in my life. In any walk of life you have to give it your best – and I always did for Preston."

Those of us who witnessed and enjoyed that 1977/78 promotion season were privileged that amid the North End ranks was perhaps the slickest striking partnership ever to pull on North End shirts in modern times.

Many thanks Alex and Mike, like many others I'm so grateful for all those wonderful memories!

Above: Mike Elwiss as I will always remember him, flying down the wing after beating a defender, looking to set up Alex Bruce

Left: The dream strike force at a PNE Former Players dinner

Bottom: Alex Bruce heads in the second of his four goals in the victory over Colchester United at Deepdale in 1977/78—the centre provided as always by Mike Elwiss...

CHAPTER 22

1978/79 COMES SHARPLY INTO FOCUS

If Nobby Stiles or Alan Kelly were expecting a quiet time immediately following the May Day promotion, they were sadly mistaken.

Monday's 'high' was soon dissipated by the news that they had been asked to 'present their ideas on which players were likely to be retained' to the board on Wednesday, 3rd May. This was code for 'there are going to be cuts', especially when Stiles told the LEP that, *"the economics of the situation are going be spelt out to us."*

Before the meeting, the board issued a statement. They told Stiles and Kelly what they needed to do. *"It was the unanimous opinion of the directors that the staff of 23 full time professionals should be reduced to 18, and this can be done without affecting in anyway the success of Preston on their return to the Second division."*

By the following day, the management pair had duly nominated five players who were basically sacked overnight – the harsh reality of life at promotion winning Preston North End! Reserve goalkeeper Alex Smith, midfielder Jimmy Brown, reserve striker Jim Campbell, reserve defender Grant Davies, and 'Young Player of the Year' defender/winger Peter Morris – quite a surprise this one – as the youngster had performed excellently in the reserve team and only just received his award from

Stiles and Kelly! The reward from the board for this frugality was swiftly proffered:-

"In view of this, the board approved the list of retained players and the proposed signing of one additional player in the close season."

No additional funds of any consequence had been introduced to the club either through direct contributions from any of the directors or any other outside source, bar the usual raffles and lotteries.

There was thankfully a good news story by the end of the week in that Alex Bruce had won the Division Three 'Golden Shoe' award for being Division Three leading scorer of 1977/78. He was to receive his honour the following week at a dinner in London, and well deserved it was too.

However, during the close season, the inevitable happened and the board of directors accepted with their usual alacrity, a bid of £200,000 for an essential cog of the North End team – captain, Mike Elwiss.

Elwiss was seemingly keen to try his hand at a larger – and more progressive – club and at his age and with his capabilities, it seemed to make perfect sense. Maybe he had realised that North End would always be between Division Two or lower, and this was his moment. Who could really blame him wanting to experience being coached by Terry Venables?

His first team colleague, Gordon Coleman recalled these times in an interview in 2013:-

"We had a good team back then. We had Mike Elwiss, Alex Bruce, John McMahon – some really good players.

"We thought we would go from strength to strength, but we started to sell our star players. Mike Elwiss went to Crystal Palace, Mark Lawrenson and Gary Williams went to Brighton.

"We were selling all these good players and not replacing them with players of similar ability"

For the fan it was gutting. Why couldn't we do what Crystal Palace or Brighton were doing?

Both had languished in Division Two and lower in the mid Sixties, even Seventies – just like North End. We had for years consistently produced top quality players who we then readily sold on without blinking just to keep the status quo policy of 'sell big, buy small' in place. It had got us precisely nowhere – and now before a ball had even been kicked in earnest in Division Two in 1978 we had peddled part of our soul – again!

We had become Preston North End – suppliers to the trade of exceptionally good players.

I swore I would never darken the door of a North End turnstile again, but that didn't last long and when the new season began I was there – strictly as a supporter of Stiles and Kelly...or so went my climbdown excuse anyway!

The new season started quite well. A 2-2 draw at Ninian Park, Cardiff was followed by a fantastic late summer evening at Deepdale three days later, when Blackburn Rovers were put to the sword by 4-1, including a brace for Alex Bruce. Another 2-2 draw then followed at Deepdale against Sheffield United before form fell away completely.

The next 10 games consisted of eight defeats and two draws, leaving North End planted at the foot of the table with just six points from 13 games. Finally, a win at home over Cardiff City on November 11th heralded a remarkable upswing in fortune. Of the next 12 games, only one would be lost and would see North End climb to mid table security.

Stiles and Kelly had devised a system which made North End hard to beat, no matter how good the opposition was. It resulted in a high tally of drawn games over the season, but with a draw having more value than today, (half of a win, rather than a third), the effect was that North End kept slowly rising up the table to eventually finish in seventh place – their highest placing since the golden 1963/64 season.

It was a remarkable feat, and a great reflection on the shrewd thought process that Stiles and Kelly had put into rescuing the season following North End's hard won promotion of a few months before. Abruptly halting a defeat percentage of 61.53 and reducing it to 13.97 enabled North End to continually amass points over the remaining 29 matches.

Preston North End Division Two performance, November 10th 1978 – May 22nd 1979

Date	Position	Pl	W	D	L	F	A	Pts	Loss %
04/11/78	21st	13	1	4	8	18	30	6	61.53%
22/05/79	7th	42	12	18	12	59	57	42	28.57%

04/11/78 – 22/05/79	29	11	14	4	41	27	36	13.79%

With the unexpected but irresistible £200k now banked by the board, Stiles was eventually allowed to bring in more than just the one player he was initially promised.

Eric Potts, a diminutive but very active striker was brought in from Brighton, followed by Irishman Don O'Riordan and Brian Taylor from Tulsa Roughnecks and Plymouth Argyle respectively to shore up a struggling defence.

Later in the season Graham Bell, a true midfield craftsman, joined the Lilywhites from Oldham Athletic just after the big signing of the season, Steve Elliott had arrived from Nottingham Forest. North End remarkably splashed out a club record fee of £95,000 for the centre forward, the board buoyed no doubt by the regular income stream from that season's increased home gates.

CHAPTER 23

1978/79

PRESTON NORTH END V BLACKBURN ROVERS
AUGUST 22ND 1978

Rovers sent packing

The 4-1 demolition of Blackburn Rovers at Deepdale in front of a crowd of 15,412 back on a balmy summer's evening in August 1978 isn't a game that easily escapes the memory.

In my entire North End watching career to that point, I had never witnessed a win over our closest rivals. In fact there had only been a two victories in the whole period from 1965 – 1978; a midweek 3-0 home win in September 1966 which I didn't see, and a victory I do recall but also wasn't present to witness, a 1-0 win at Ewood on Easter Saturday 1968 when a converted Willie Irvine penalty left our friends choking on their chocolate Easter eggs.

It had been too nice a day to be working, but I had been and I was really looking forward to being entertained after 'wolfing' my tea down following the day's travails. I parked up my car near the Sumners and walked down to the ground, hoping for the best after a decent point had been gleaned from the opening day visit to Ninian Park; Alex Bruce starting the campaign in fine style with a brace of goals.

North End lined up:-

Tunks, Cameron, Wilson, Doyle, Baxter, Cross, Burns, Haselgrave, Robinson, Thomson, Bruce. Substitute: Smith

Before the game even got into full swing, North End were one down. The referee had apparently blown for a handball against Danny Cameron just outside the North End box giving the visitors a free kick. Tony Parkes slipped the ball neatly to Stuart Metcalfe whose snap shot struck the crossbar before bouncing into play again where striker David Gregory was on hand to loop a header back over Roy Tunks and then watch the ball bounce in for the opener. Urgh! Definitely not the start the now silenced North End fans had wanted!

Unlike several North Ends of old, this particular team grasped the match by the throat and took the game to Rovers with immediate effect. Showing confidence in both passing and movement North End equalised after around 10 minutes after a move down the right that saw Bruce lay the ball off nicely to Francis Burns who instantly crossed a low ball into the Rovers box. Michael Robinson, careering in and leaving marker Glen Keeley in his wake, crashed the moving ball home past Rovers 'keeper John Butcher without pausing for thought.

It was a great strike and no more than North End deserved. Robinson looked like he had filled out a little more in the close season but this hadn't affected his mobility.

The dominance continued unabated. Shots rained in on Butcher's goal as North End piled on the pressure with constructive and destructive play. Any type of move that Rovers tried to cobble together was broken up almost immediately as North End didn't let the visitors settle into any pattern. The North End midfield was 'on fire' with Ricky Thomson, Sean Haselgrave, Stephen Doyle and Burns contributing heavily.

The flying Roy Tunks cannot stop Stuart Metcalfe's snap shot hitting the crossbar...

...or prevent David Gregory's header looping into the net from the rebound

Indeed, it was Doyle who put North End ahead mid-way through the first half. The roving Bruce, this time cutting in from the left found the Welshman around 18 yards out and centrally placed in the penalty area.

The youngster made no mistake as he firmly side footed the ball home beneath the diving Butcher, much to the Kop's – and all the other North End fans – delight.

The home dominance continued unabated, and Rovers did well to desperately bat away everything that came their way in the remaining 20 minutes or so of the first half.

After Metcalfe had limped off to be replaced by Noel Brotherston, there was a great piece of interplay between Thomson and Haselgrave, the dashing move culminating in a rocket like shot from Robinson that went just over the bar.

North End were warmly applauded off the pitch when the referee drew a veil over proceedings at 45 minutes; the talking point at half time was just how many goals North End would put away in the second half.

Alex Bruce lashes the ball into the net to score North End's third

Robinson set the tone within a minute of the restart, when he swooped down to head inches wide from a cross by Haselgrave. Harry Wilson was then booked for a foul on Gregory after Rovers surprisingly strayed over the half way line into North End territory, but within a couple of minutes Rovers were left fighting for air after the phenomenal Bruce struck Preston's third.

Rovers defender Kevin Hird failed miserably with his attempt to control the ball in midfield and Thomson seized the opportunity to intercept and immediately send Bruce away down the right. The goal-machine shimmied his man, cut inside and started to hurtle his way towards the Rovers box.

Just as he reached the perimeter of the box with defender John Bailey now in tow, Bruce launched a torpedo like shot courtesy of his left boot that flew past the diving Butcher and rebounded off the far post and into the net. What a goal! Needless to say a deafening roar engulfed Deepdale for the third time that evening. The Rovers defenders were all stood there looking at each other, hands on hips.

Rovers regathered and started again. For the next 20 minutes or so, they held their own. They created no real goal opportunities however, but at least they stemmed the goal flow towards their own end. Their best attempt in this period was when Gregory swiveled and fired in a quick shot that Tunks was easily able to parry and Mick Baxter clear effortlessly back downfield.

With around 15 minutes of the game left, North End sprang to life again to put the result beyond all reasonable doubt.

Thomson swung the ball in from a corner on the right, and Burns headed the ball on in the direction of goal. Butcher reached the ball awkwardly and only managed to pat the ball down into an area of heavy traffic as he fell towards the ground. The ball bounced around and eventually presented itself to Bruce who fired in from point blank range. Again Butcher got his body in the way, but Bruce wasn't going to be denied a second time.

As the ball bounced out once again, he hammered a vicious shot into the roof of the net from about four yards out, before turning to accept the 'hugs and kisses' of his teammates and the cheers of the crowd.

North End, with two prospective signings watching on from the Pavilion Stand – West Bromwich Albion's Mick Martin and Brighton's Eric Potts – couldn't have impressed their guests more.

Despite further attempts from John Smith (on the pitch to replace the injured Cameron), Baxter and Bruce, the game ended 4-1 and the Lilywhites were cheered all the way back down the tunnel after the final whistle.

North End's fourth goal is crashed into the net from point blank range by Alex Bruce

The LEP reported that Stiles was smiling like a 'PNE lottery winner' after the match, saying:-

"All the lads played very well and passed the ball around accurately. Bruce was very sharp indeed and could knock goals in on an ice rink."

For me, the fascination was Michael Robinson. I had never seen anybody work as hard for North End over 90 minutes since Archie Gemmill a decade before. He already had the makings of being a tremendous centre forward football-wise, but somehow he had added an enduring brutal strength and stamina to his game which meant his engine now maintained full effort over the whole match, never faltering in the process.

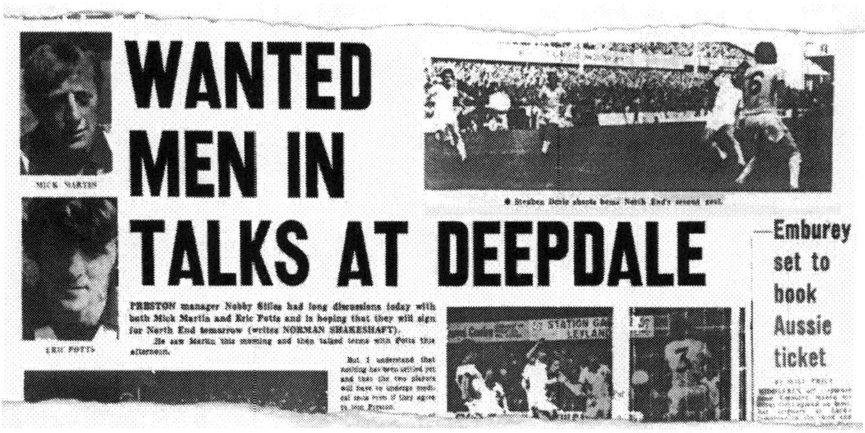

MICK MARTIN

ERIC POTTS

WANTED MEN IN TALKS AT DEEPDALE

PRESTON manager Nobby Stiles had long discussions today with both Mick Martin and Eric Potts and is hoping that they will sign for North End tomorrow (writes NORMAN SHAKESHAFT).

He saw Martin this morning and then talked terms with Potts this afternoon.

But, I understand that nothing has been settled yet and that the two players will have to undergo medical tests even if they agree to join Preston.

Emburey set to book Aussie ticket

In the event, Mick Martin received a better offer from Newcastle United, but Eric Potts completed his move to Deepdale the following day

CHAPTER 24

1978/79

PRESTON NORTH END V DERBY COUNTY
FA CUP 3RD ROUND, JANUARY 16TH 1979

Doc despatched

The weather early in the new year of 1979 was dreadful. Heavy snow countrywide which then froze hard under clear skies led to the usual transport chaos. Football was hit particularly hard, and there were hundreds of postponements the length and breadth of the nation.

The third round of the FA Cup had paired North End and Division One Derby County together with the tie scheduled for Saturday, January 6th at Deepdale. The contest finally took place on Tuesday, January 16th – and was the first outing for both teams in 1979.

The last time the Tommy Docherty had visited Deepdale in a management capacity was with Aston Villa in 1969, when his team's boorish play and blatant time wasting tactics coupled with his post match comments lost him much respect in this part of the world.

Before this contest, his comments about North End were complimentary. Derby would have to be on their guard he warned as,

"Preston are no mugs."

Both teams stood in 16th position in their respective divisions, neither in any imminent danger of being involved in a relegation fight. It wasn't league form that mattered though on this occasion – and North End could point to a bit of history in turning over 'bigger clubs' who had been drawn to travel to Deepdale.

Walking towards the ground from the Sumners was an exercise in keeping upright. Although a thaw of sorts had started, the pavement still looked like it had a very thick sheet of rough glass bonded to it, so I like many others – spirits lifted by a pre-match pint of Bodd's – walked on the gritted road. It was a harmless necessity and I'm sure that those people in their warm cars understood the dilemma fully ...well one or two of them anyway ...as the wall of fans finally 'gave way' fully to the traffic build up behind them at the Blackpool Road junction!

There was a real air of expectation about the match after being starved of football for almost three weeks and this was reflected in the excellent attendance figure of 19,901.

Docherty had already pronounced that County would be at full strength, and Nobby Stiles was in a position to do much the same. North End lined up:-

Tunks, Taylor, Cameron, Burns, Baxter, O'Riordan, Coleman, Haselgrave, Robinson, Potts, Bruce. Substitute: Doyle

That North End line up was an admirable blend of youth and experience, balanced and above all talented. There was even an 'ankle biter' warming the bench if needed!

The match kicked off to a massive roar, with North End attacking the Kop – and attack they did; so much so that by the time County fell behind after six minutes, they hadn't crossed the half way line into North End's half. The Lilywhites had run the Rams off their feet and the tactic had paid off handsomely.

Michael Robinson, all energetic power and forward propulsion won a corner on the right. Francis Burns ran across to take the kick as North End prepared to play a move they regularly used around this time. It was fantastically uncomplicated in that it utilised Mick Baxter's height and Alex Bruce's finishing ability. Burns floated the ball into the box and placed it perfectly for Baxter to run, leap at, and head the ball on across the goalmouth whereupon Bruce brought the ball under control and slammed it beyond goalkeeper David McKellar and into the net. It was a great start, and due reward for North End's sustained early onslaught.

Alex Bruce fires North End into an early lead against Division One Derby County

Preston kept up the pressure, but gradually Derby settled down in midfield and started engineering a move or two of their own. Winger Gordon Hill, who was with Docherty at Manchester United, was a beneficiary of this, breaking free to centre for Jon Clark (who would play for North End in the Eighties), but he headed over from 10 yards.

A Derby corner then whistled across the face of goal begging to be directed into the North End net before Don O'Riordan was lectured for a foul on Clark and then booked for another on midfielder and Eire international, Gerry Daly.

This was Derby's best spell of the match, and the second of two corners in quick succession caused real consternation in the North End goalmouth after Roy Tunks lost possession of the ball as he fell to the ground. The ball fell to defender David Webb (ex-Chelsea), but he wasted the opportunity by blasting the ball high and wide.

Michael Robinson about to clear the ball following a header by County's Steve Powell

Midfielder Steve Carter then delighted the crowd with a display of histrionics claiming to the officials that he had been felled. Ignoring the referee's decision to play on, Carter then confronted Mr. Seel who calmly reached for his book while the rant was in progress.

With half time almost upon us, Hill – who had been making signals to the Derby bench for five minutes or so – was replaced by former 'Spurs centre forward John Duncan.

While under this Derby pressure, North End never gave up running and harrying the visitors, and just about deserved to be in the lead at half time.

North End began the second half as they had started the first – on all-out attack. Derby, or should I say Docherty, was ready for this and had obviously told his charges to nip any form of North End onslaught in the bud with heavy tackles. It was his management style, unfortunately.

Former England international Roy McFarland set the tone when he was instantly booked for kicking Gordon Coleman. The fouling continued; Bruce was the next to suffer badly when he was hacked down by Clark from behind as he was breaking clear. Robinson then lifted the spirits with a fine trademark run, hustling and bustling through the Derby defence before being robbed at the vital moment by right back David Langan.

Don O'Riordan heads the ball clear following a Derby County attack

In the meantime, Webb had been noticeably limping for quite some time and was hanging around the touchline near the player's tunnel in conversation with Docherty and the trainer. The upshot of this was that Docherty came to the touchline, waved his arms around and Steve Powell, in the Derby midfield, made his way into the visitors back line. Webb, was left for the remainder of the game limping along the right wing.

It didn't take North End long to start dominating proceedings, now that they were effectively playing against 10 men. Clark and Eric Potts then traded wide shots, before Sean Haselgrave made himself some room and skimmed a shot just over the bar.

It wasn't long before North End took full advantage and doubled their lead. It would be nice to be able to describe an intricate piece of build-up play, but unfortunately not this time – but what a goal!

Latching onto a Derby loose ball, O'Riordan, intending to play the ball wide completely sliced the ball down the middle of the field. The visitor's back line was high and caught completely flat footed, as Bruce took control of the ball and started to run forward. Up the arms went for offside, but the linesman kept his flag down and continued his run down the line in tandem with Bruce.

Alex Bruce increases North End's lead with a brilliant individual goal

Suddenly out of nothing, Bruce – now joined by the speedy Potts – was being roared on as he approached the Town End goal with only David McKellar in front of him. The noise level dropped as McKellar raced forward from his line for the moment of confrontation. Bruce maintained his composure and at the very moment the goalkeeper hinted he was diving to his left, Bruce dipped his left shoulder, taking the ball around the powerless McKellar before passing it into the empty net ...without any trouble whatsoever.

The massive roar then returned! As the ground shook with delight at such a wonderfully taken goal, Bruce's teammates were leaping around the pitch in sheer joy.

There was just less than ten minutes remaining as Derby restarted, rushing forward in what was a call-to-arms of forlorn hope. There was no way they were going to level this encounter, let alone win it and it was Burns, who finally slammed down the lid on any such miracle.

Throughout the match Robinson had showcased his strength and power on a very heavy surface, and true to nature he went wide down the right with just five minutes remaining on a seemingly meandering lone journey, shrugging off challenges for possession of the ball along the way. Then, showing quality and maturity way beyond his 20 years, he impeccably timed a pass to meet the conclusion of Burns' 30 yard dash forward down the middle; the classy midfielder lashing home a left foot shot to seal an outstanding win.

For Burns, who had orchestrated North End throughout, it was a well deserved reward. Shortly after Robinson flashed a header over the bar a couple of minutes later, the referee blew for time.

Quite rightly, North End were cheered off the pitch for their efforts and in terms of a decade that had seen them go out of the competition early including an exit at non-league Scarborough just a few years previously, it was a welcome return to their historic traditions in the FA Cup.

After the game, Stiles was full of praise for his North End team and in particular, Bruce.

"Alex Bruce showed how he can knock the ball in and he is a great player to work with. It is said by reporters that he failed in Division One at Newcastle but that isn't true – he only left there because he was

unhappy.

"He will score goals at any level and I could not place a price on him even if I was prepared to sell him."

So proud of Preston

North End heroes plough through the mud to gain an emphatic victory

PRESTON can be proud of the North End heroes who ploughed through the mud and outran, outfought and outlasted the First Division men from Derby County at Deepdale last night to gain an emphatic 3-0 win in the FA Cup third round game sponsored by the "Lancashire Evening Post."

North End's reward is a fourth round home game against another First Division club, Southampton, on January 22, and the Saints will have to come marching in at their best to beat Preston if the North End players show the same spirit as they did last night.

Certainly, Derby, who had not played since Boxing Day, could not match Second Division Preston in effort and enthusiasm — and finished well beaten.

DOC ADMITS: THE BEST TEAM WON!

Pictures by ROY PAYNE and BERNARD HOWE

Docherty too had kind words to say about North End unlike on the occasion of his last visit, when manager of Aston Villa in 1969.

"Preston impressed me with their fighting spirit. I'm disappointed with the result, but North End fully deserved their win."

CHAPTER 25

1978/79

PRESTON NORTH END V SOUTHAMPTON FA CUP 4TH ROUND, FEBRUARY 12TH 1979

Ball settles his 'grudge'

Following Preston's deserved win over Derby County in the FA Cup on January 16th, the harsh weather conditions continued nationwide. North End wouldn't see match action of any type for almost a month.

Deepdale then hosted two matches in three days. A good win over Division Two table toppers Brighton on Saturday, February 10th was quickly followed by the FA Cup fourth round tie against Southampton two days later on the Monday evening.

Originally pencilled in for January 27th, the tie was now just over two weeks overdue, but this was by no means the worst case. The two final ties of the fourth round were played on February 26th, one of which went to a replay, played on March 1st! February and March were indeed the months of 'overlapping rounds' and as the weather eased, remarkably both the semi-finals were played on the originally allocated date of March 31st.

Southampton, like Derby County were at the time a lower mid table team in Division One. Managed by the genial Lawrie McMenemy, they had only been promoted back to the top tier at the end of the previous season, but by the time of the match at Deepdale had already battled through to the forthcoming final of the League Cup. As far as the FA Cup was concerned, they had actually lifted the trophy in May 1976, beating Manchester United 1-0 with a goal from Bobby Stokes. They certainly had some cup pedigree.

During the extended build up to the game, it emerged that Southampton's midfield general, Alan Ball, was determined to knock North End out of the competition as retribution for his father's sacking six years before.

His memories of that day had remained vivid. He had to race up the motorway to help his father clear his office and take him back home to Farnworth as the Preston directors had demanded the keys to his North End car to be returned immediately. Such crass insensitivity from the board was petty, ridiculous and downright embarrassing. It had certainly left its mark on the former England captain.

"It was one of the saddest days of my life, and I have never forgiven the Preston directors for what they did to my father. You don't easily forget having to help him pack up because they wouldn't let him use the car. I just want to beat North End for his sake.

"To think of a man as keen and enthusiastic about football as him whiling away his time in Swedish football is a crime."

I remember wincing at those articles at the time, and I winced again when I dug them out whilst preparing this book. It added an unnecessary edge to the game and was the start of a long hate relationship between sections of the North End crowd and Ball Jnr for many years to come.

His father was treated shabbily by North End and not just on that final day – but the majority of the Preston fans had stood firmly behind his dad at the time of his sacking. However, some of them unfortunately took Ball Jnr's words personally and made him a target of abuse, which wasn't really necessary. I had seen him play for England, Everton and Arsenal and he had shown enough class on the pitch to be afforded some respect. Unfortunately the opposite occurred whenever he came to Deepdale after he revealed this long standing grudge.

Nobby Stiles meanwhile had obviously read about all this in the newspapers but would not be drawn into making any comment about it. *"What Ballie says is up to him,"* he explained, *"I am not concerned with it. All I know is that he is one of the best players in the country, and we will have to play even better than we did against Derby County to beat Southampton."*

Match ticket for the FA Cup tie against Southampton at Deepdale, bearing the date when the match should have originally been played

The final ironic twist in this saga – the clash against Southampton now rearranged for February 12th, was exactly six years to the day since Alan Ball Snr was sacked…

It was a cold, brisk walk down the hill from the Sumners to Deepdale. There was so much traffic at the Blackpool Road junction with Deepdale Road that people were milling around the cars everywhere and this was reflected when the attendance was later confirmed as 20,727 – North End's biggest crowd for some time.

Stiles named the same team for the seventh consecutive time:-

Tunks, Taylor, Cameron, Burns, Baxter, O'Riordan, Coleman, Haselgrave, Robinson, Potts, Bruce. Substitute: Doyle

The match began and despite the best efforts of the home fans, they couldn't lift a sluggish North End opening. As the half wore on it was obvious that the Saints' mixture of experience and talented youth was the cause of North End's lack of impact rather than any lack of effort from the Lilywhites.

For Southampton, Chris Nicholl the captain and centre half was prominent at the back, organising and prompting whenever necessary. Similarly, Ball was putting on a fine show in midfield, and his ability to pass and move was stretching the North End midfield far and wide.

North End weren't helped by the fact that their passing wasn't accurate enough when it counted as Alex Bruce (twice), and Michael Robinson found to their cost after finding the necessary space. Around 20 minutes in, the visitors went ahead. The goal was scored by Ball...

Alex Bruce stretches but just fails to connect with this Eric Potts cross

Southampton had won a corner on the left and it was swung in by Nick Holmes. Roy Tunks only half punched the ball away into the penalty area whereupon Chris Nicholl and then Trevor Hebberd both had shots charged down by the desperate North End defence. Malcolm Waldron then smartly turned the rebound to into the path of Ball who cut in from the left of the penalty area to crash in a perfect angled shot that flew in to the roof of the net.

The unremitting barracking that Ball had received to that point was silenced for a few minutes at least as he celebrated with his teammates. It resumed the very next time he touched the ball.

Alan Ball strikes the only goal of the game following mayhem in the North End box

Worryingly, the visitors didn't show any indications of sitting back on their one goal lead, and further moments of anguish were suffered by the home fans as efforts by Ball, Waldron, Terry Curran and Phil Boyer all went close. North End in contrast could only point to a Francis Burns shot that went over the crossbar, a cross from Eric Potts that Bruce failed to reach, and closest of all – a Ball back pass that almost eluded goalkeeper Terry Gennoe as it trickled towards the goal line bringing more loud howls of derision from the home crowd.

The second half began with a flurry of activity from North End. Only a brave diving save by Gennoe at the feet of Robinson foiled the rampaging forward as he thundered towards the Town End goal, and five minutes later Gennoe was out very smartly again diving low to parry away a powerful Bruce drive at point blank range.

This gave the home fans some hope at last, but gradually Southampton started to control matters again and move the play to Preston's half despite the best efforts of Burns, who was enjoying another good performance.

Top: Terry Gennoe bravely dives at the feet of the rampaging Michael Robinson

Bottom: A shot from Alex Bruce is smothered by Gennoe as North End push forward

Back came North End though and the visitors had cause once again to thank Gennoe, as his quick thinking and dash forward intercepted a dangerous pass from Sean Haselgrave that Eric Potts was making rapid progress towards. Indeed, it was Haselgrave's screaming shot that next had the North End fans cheering loudly, as it passed over Gennoe's crossbar by inches.

North End continued to huff and puff but in reality were kept at arm's length by a very smart Southampton outfit. They patently had too much for North End, and this was confirmed by Stiles after the game. *"We knew Southampton were a very good team and they proved it, but I'm not too disappointed with the result because we came back well after the interval. In the first half some of the lads were overawed."*

"Ballie? He's still England class."

McMenemy had some kind words for North End. *"Preston battled really well in the second half, so much so that we couldn't relax. We could and should have had more goals in the first half when we were in control of the game."*

Ball was asked about his take on matters too. *"I thought of my dad when my goal went in. I heard the fans barracking me, but that didn't bother me as I was more concerned about putting one over on Preston."*

With that, interest in the FA Cup was ended for another season. We would have to wait another eight long years to participate in the fourth round again, by then under the guidance of John McGrath.

CHAPTER 26

1978/79

PRESTON NORTH END V FULHAM
MARCH 3RD 1979

Robinson starts to blossom

After exiting the FA Cup at the hands of Southampton, North End had another break due to the continuing weather problems (12 days), then resumed action and played both Crystal Palace and Stoke City away from home. Both clubs were serious promotion contenders; but the Stiles/Kelly tactics that had transformed North End into a team that was difficult to put to the sword ensured that North End brought a valuable point home from each fixture, continuing their slow rise up the table to 13th position.

The next home game was against Fulham, a team on the periphery of the promotion chasing pack. The match was played in dull and cold conditions, and I include this contest as it was on this day I realised why Michael Robinson would become a prize asset.

It was still the days of un-segregated crowds, and I had chosen a spot in the Pavilion Paddock towards the Town End roughly in line with the penalty spot. For the 20 minutes or so before kick-off I stood virtually alone, but as the teams ran out I was surrounded by around 30 or so Fulham fans, a mix of parents and young children who had seemingly travelled up north together. They were a friendly, civilised bunch; whenever they needed to know something about the ground or a player, they politely tapped me on the shoulder and I would enlighten them. Ah, the good old days...

With Francis Burns still injured, Nobby Stiles continued with Stephen Doyle, fielding the same line-up for the second time in succession:-

Tunks, Taylor, Cameron, Doyle, Baxter, O'Riordan, Coleman, Haselgrave, Robinson, Potts, Bruce. Substitute: Wilson

From the evidence of the pre-match kick about, the pitch looked very heavy – unsurprising really after endless weeks of rotations of the snow-ice-thaw cycle.

Fulham, in an all red strip to avoid a colour clash had been flashing the cash, looking to move onwards and upwards. They had signed five new players for this campaign at a total outlay of £385,000 but were pinned back from the start by an energetic looking North End. Slick movement from the Lilywhites abounded, and a lovely move involving Sean Haselgrave, Alex Bruce and Robinson ended when the big centre forward shot wide. North End were on a roll and after Gordon Coleman fired in a cross, Bruce hit a spectacular shot that hit the bar and cannoned away for a goal kick.

The first tap on the shoulder came at this point. "Do Preston always start this quick? We ain't touched the ball yet!" asked a middle aged chap. I replied cautiously, "Frustratingly, only sometimes," and he saw the funny side of that. "My name's Pete by the way," he replied, offering his hand to shake.

The formalities over, attention was drawn back to the game as the crowd's noise level suddenly rose. A scramble in the visitor's goalmouth ended when the loose ball was fed back to Doyle some 30 yards out, whereupon the youngster launched an almighty first time shot at the Fulham goal, that goalkeeper Gerry Peyton did well hold onto.

North End were swarming all over Fulham like a disturbed nest of ants, and they crowned this sparkling start by taking the lead on 10 minutes. The reliable Brian Taylor pounded down the right wing and centred the ball into the Fulham goalmouth. Robinson went up with the goalkeeper to challenge for the ball and incredibly leapt as high as Peyton's fingertips could stretch to, calmly nodding the ball backwards into the path of Bruce who although surrounded by defenders, managed to lob the ball into the net.

Second tap on the shoulder. "Who the bloody hell is the big boy that won the header? I missed the game against your lot back home."

"That's Robinson," I replied "He's rapidly developing into a very good player."

"I'll say. See that header? Class. What a big boy he is – strong. Where did you get him from?"

"Came through the youth system..." My new acquaintance pursed his lips, shook his head and then said, "Wow," which I took to mean how lucky we were.

Fulham were rattled enough by now to actually try and move into the North End half, and it was (although we didn't know it then), our old friend John Beck who split the defence open with a through ball that centre forward Chris Guthrie latched onto forcing Roy Tunks into making his first save of the day.

The pitch was cutting up badly by now, but despite this both teams were dealing with it reasonably well. There was a false alarm following another North End assault on goal when Peyton could only parry a Bruce shot into the path of Coleman who drilled the ball straight back into the net; the loud cheers of the home fans silenced when they realised that Eric Potts had been pulled for offside.

Peyton was very busy. Continually assailed by North End from all directions, he was called upon to make to saves in quick succession when, after diving to block a good shot from Potts, he had to run out of his penalty area to thwart the rapidly approaching Robinson who was following Doyle's through ball.

"The runaway train came over the hill and she blew..." said my new mate Pete acknowledging the rampant Robinson's never say die attitude.

Shortly afterwards, North End scored again. Another exquisite through ball from Doyle found another of North End's willing forward runners – this time Potts. Picking the ball up in his stride the little striker glided forward, drew Peyton, and fired the ball over the 'keeper's dive. It was a lovely goal; superb football all round.

Eric Potts scores North End's second goal

A word here about Eric Potts – he once walked into my dad's hardware shop to buy some decorating materials whist I happened to be there. After my shock had worn off, he actually chatted with me for about 20 minutes about North End, Nobby, Brighton, Alan Mullery and football in general. What a lovely bloke!

Preston continued to attack, and Robinson drove forward at pace down the wing to fire in a hard low centre across the face of goal that tantalisingly just missed Bruce's outstretched boot. Doyle was then booked for dissent after being pulled up for a foul but responded by slicing open the Fulham defence yet again with a pass that the ever willing Robinson latched on to; his shot being saved by Peyton.

Fulham had been manfully plugging way without being damaging in any way to North End, but then conjured up a goal from nowhere; 'conjured' being the operative word! It was credited to striker Peter Kitchen, but according to any North End player you would care to ask who was playing that day, the ball never actually crossed the line.

From my vantage point it seemed that following a Fulham free kick, Kevin Lock shot at goal, the ball deflected off a North End defender and into the path of Kitchen whose first attempt hit the base of the post and his second prod at the ball had seemingly taken the ball over the goal line.

Despite some protests from a few of the North End players, the 'goal' stood and the score at half time was 2-1.

Later it emerged that the North End players involved all agreed the ball never crossed the goal line. Preston's viewpoint was that Kitchen's first attempt – which had little power, hit the post after which the ball nestled dead on the line. Robinson then scooped the ball away whilst falling over, the ball then came straight back again, now amid a tangle of bodies. The ball again gently makes it to the line, whereupon the boot of Danny Cameron finally clears it away.

Indeed, full back Cameron was adamant maintaining, *"The ball went along the line, never over it."*

Meanwhile, my new friend Pete was waxing lyrical about North End's performance. He got onto the subject of Robinson again and I shared with him my thoughts that his massive strength and stamina were tremendous assets and that he would go far.

Pete then revealed, "Well, I used to do some scouting at schools level for Fulham, and believe me mate if I had spotted him for them it would have been like hitting the jackpot! Just been speaking to my mate about him; has anybody been in for him yet?"

I said not that I knew of, but at Preston if they have talent they aren't around long – which caused a bit of a laugh all round.

The match resumed, and I was hoping that Fulham would remain as generally anonymous as they had been in the first half. In fact, it started out just like that. Cameron launched a long cross into the Fulham box which caused a certain degree of strife, before Haselgrave shot just over the bar after the ball eventually ran free.

Fulham inched forward, and after progressing to the edge of the box Lock curled in a dangerous cross on the run that eluded Kitchen by a whisker as it flew across the face of Tunks' goal.

Michael Robinson, pictured against Burnley, displaying his usual enthusiastic attitude

North End replied indignantly and Potts embarked on a fine forward run, passing the ball to Coleman at the sweetest moment. The midfielder's 20 yard drive looked a contender for 'Goal of the Season' all the way until Peyton somehow tipped it around the post for a corner, much to the home fans' annoyance. The corner was swung in, only tentatively cleared and Bruce's shot hit the net…but frustratingly on the wrong side of the post.

North End were approaching full swing again by now, and Doyle, still in control of midfield, launched another wonderful through ball to the willing workhorse Robinson, whose backbreaking efforts to reach the ball on the now ploughed surface led to the winning of a corner, and huge roars of approval from the crowd.

It was like a scene from the Royal Marines devised fitness section of *'The Krypton Factor,'* a popular weekly television contest of the time that tested mind and body. Robinson's efforts that day for his team were nothing less than superhuman. What a shift he put in!

Out on the Fulham wing was the ex-Arsenal hope, Peter Marinello. Somehow it had never quite worked out for the Scot after his move to the capital and sadly, many more troubles and his personal nadir were still well ahead of him at this time.

It was from a hoofed Fulham clearance that he sprung into action, taking on and beating three North End defenders on a long mission towards their penalty area, before Taylor finally halted his progress at the cost of a corner. Thankfully this came to nothing, but at least I had got a glimpse of Marinello's capabilities.

Preston stormed back and won two corners in quick succession; Potts having a shot brilliantly saved from the second.

At around this time, Bobby Campbell the Fulham manager switched two players around. Lock fell back into the defensive line while Tony Gale was pushed up into midfield. It paid dividends as they finally gained a foothold in the middle, and suddenly looked a polished outfit befitting their league position.

North End continued to go forward looking for the clincher but it continued to elude them, epitomised when Mick Baxter rose and firmly headed a Coleman centre that scraped the Fulham crossbar with Peyton rooted to the ground.

Peyton was then booked for rushing out of his area and handling the ball rather than let Bruce pick up Coleman's pass when the Fulham defence was caught completely flat footed. Don O'Riordan headed over from the free kick, and time was almost up.

It was to be one of those 'twist of fate' days for North End. Despite making all the running in the contest playing wonderful football along the way, they were undone in the 90th minute by simplicity itself.

Kitchen received a short forward pass from midfield, headed to the right and fed the ball to Ray Evans moving down the right wing. The full back's cross was met perfectly by centre forward Guthrie, whose header passed Tunks like an arrow. The goal came as a massive anti-climax for the home fans, who had witnessed an excellent performance from their team.

"Never rule out the numpties," said Pete as I turned to leave. "We didn't deserve a bean there. Listen mate, nice to talk to you today and I'll be looking out for the big lad (Robinson) in future." Unfortunately we still had two years to wait before the dawning of Derek 'Del-Boy' Trotter, otherwise I would have almost certainly have replied, "Cushty."

Newspaper reports over the weekend suggested that North End secretary Derek Allen, in another part of the building even overheard Campbell's no-holds-barred half time rollicking to his troops. He later said, *"We lifted our game in the second half, but our defence and midfield vastly improved after switching Lock and Gale."*

Stiles praised his team. *"We were magnificent in the first half and this after a strenuous midweek game at Stoke. I'm delighted with the manner in which we played the game, even though Fulham were able to hang on in the game after being hammered."*

For me, like my Fulham friends, it was Robinson who was the stand out North End performer. Indomitable, resolute, determined, muscular and spirited – Michael Robinson encompassed them all.

CHAPTER 27

1978/79

BLACKBURN ROVERS V PRESTON NORTH END
MARCH 24TH 1979

A rare 'double'

It was just like the proverbial wait at the bus stop. You wait years to see North End beat Blackburn Rovers, and then it happens twice in a season!

To be scrupulously fair, this wasn't a classic match with Rovers struggling at the foot of the division . It was a dogged derby, but the fact that North End took the points put them – and more importantly their long suffering fans – in a good place. A crowd of 17,790 rolled up to Ewood Park to witness a contest which also saw Graham Bell don the North End strip for the first time since his arrival from Oldham Athletic.

For those younger readers who follow North End today and were not around to see this game, I have some additional information. Another 15 years had to pass before Rovers would become known as *'The Plastics'*, the term of affection used today by the vast majority of North End's fans.

As I understand it, it relates to their tens of thousands of new 'fans' who suddenly emerged from the woodwork and pledged their 'lasting allegiance' to the Rovers cause when they lifted the Premier League in 1994/95. Catapulted from Division Two obscurity with funds provided by steel magnate Jack Walker, this new wave of support had no roots or loyalty to the club whatsoever, they were just riding on a vehicle called 'bandwagon.' When it all started to go wrong they disappeared into thin air, hence they weren't real fans – they were 'plastic.'

The teams ran out on to the pitch to a loud crescendo of the North End hit number, *'Come On You Yellows'* which was bellowed out by a large contingent of Preston fans suffocating any greeting the home fans had for their team.

Apart from Bell, replacing the suspended Sean Haselgrave, Steve Elliott was starting his second game for North End after making his debut the previous weekend at Deepdale against West Ham United. With Michael Robinson languishing on the injured list, the team line-up was:-

Tunks, Taylor, Cameron, Doyle, Baxter, O'Riordan, Coleman, Bell, Elliott, Potts, Bruce. Substitute: Cochrane

North End kicked off on a cool, sunny but very windy Lancashire spring afternoon. The pitch was certainly flat but almost bereft of any grass – a victim no doubt of the long, harsh winter.

A bright start was made by both teams, but North End made the first serious progress of the afternoon when neat interplay between Brian Taylor and Alex Bruce down the right resulted in a throw-in for the Lilywhites, level with the Rovers penalty area. Bell hurled in a long throw which was neatly flicked on by Elliott, but Eric Potts couldn't take the ball under control and it was hacked away.

North End were certainly the more likely team to score in this early period and it was Gordon Coleman who set off the next raid with a neat ball to Bruce on the left of the penalty area. Surrounded by defenders, the striker still managed a return pass to Coleman, whose cross found

Bell just beyond the back post. Falling backwards, his header lacked power and was easily collected by Rovers goalkeeper Neil Ramsbottom.

Rovers then got lucky after a Bell pass backwards to Taylor was under hit, allowing Duncan McKenzie to cross the ball quickly into the North End danger area. The ball was hooked away by Stephen Doyle but Tony Parkes was on hand to control the ball and hammer a snap shot back towards the North End goal that Roy Tunks had to dive full length to halt.

North End then stunned the home fans by taking the lead after around 10 minutes.

It all began with a long clearing ball from Danny Cameron, which was headed back by Tim Parkin straight into the midfield area, by now heavily populated by advancing North Enders. Potts collected the ball and moving swiftly across field, passed to Taylor before tracking forward towards the Rovers penalty area.

Gordon Coleman was excellent in midfield for North End

Taylor then moved the ball on to Bell, who immediately launched a 40 yard diagonal cross at some pace in the direction of Bruce moving towards the straight edge of the penalty area 'D.' Within the blink of the eye, Bruce met the ball and somehow executed an incredible airborne volley on the turn that changed the direction of the ball by 90 degrees. The ball entered the bottom corner of the net before Ramsbottom had completed his dive, such was the timing of the shot. This was Bruce's 23rd goal of the season – what a perennial performer he was!

North End confidently continued to attack, but in the 15th minute all their good work was nearly undone following a calamitous defensive mix-up between Cameron and Tunks.

An over hit through ball by Parkes was guided back towards goalkeeper Tunks by Cameron who had his back towards the field of play. Unbeknown to him, McKenzie was haring in behind and when alerted to the danger he prodded the ball beyond Tunks, causing a real tangle.

McKenzie was unlucky not to cash in; the ball then bounced across the empty box towards the advancing Noel Brotherston while Cameron and Tunks hastily tried to resume position in front of goal. Brotherston's shot eluded Tunks, but Cameron was right behind him and hooked the ball off the line for a corner. Phew!

Alex Bruce stuns Ewood Park by giving North End the lead with a brilliant strike

From the resulting flag kick, the ball ran free of the box but was beautifully drilled back towards the right hand bottom corner of North End's net by Stuart Metcalfe – Tunks diving to save the ball dead on the goal line.

A strong forward header from Baxter launched another North End attack, the ball claimed in midfield by Coleman who swept a lovely ball forward to Bruce on the left. Heavily marked, the North End striker turned Rovers' loanee Mick Rathbone neatly, then progressed forward a few yards before hitting a curling shot at goal that goalkeeper Ramsbottom held on to gratefully.

Brotherston then sent the unpredictable McKenzie dashing forward but he was stopped in his tracks by Coleman who calmly hooked the ball from under the strikers feet with such élan that he managed to regain his balance then dribble past three Rovers players directly in front of him! It was an excellent piece of play and the North End midfielder was having a good game.

On the stroke of half time, Rovers put together their best move of the half when Metcalfe set Rathbone away down the right with a neat through ball. The right back turned neatly inside Cameron's challenge and lifted a testing left foot cross into the North End goalmouth. Striker Joe Craig met the ball well, but the header went wide of the near post.

The second half commenced, with Rovers more dominant than before the break.

Metcalfe was becoming more prominent, and Doyle resorted to fouling the Rovers midfielder as a move developed dangerously. The free kick came to nothing, but it was clear that North End were having difficulty creating chances now, and starting to miss the injured Michael Robinson, the willing workhorse of the forward line.

Rovers continued to probe and almost equalised in the 51st minute. John Bailey threw the ball down the left touchline to find McKenzie, who with back to goal performed a delightful turn on Taylor and launched a measured, curling cross towards the back post where Parkes was waiting unmarked.

The Rovers club captain somehow failed to control the ball but managed to get his fluffed shot beyond the sprawling Tunks. At this point Don O'Riordan intercepted with a hefty swing of the boot and incredibly the ball eventually settled in the lap of Roy Tunks, after taking a vicious, but cushioned philanthropic deflection from Parkes' meat and two veg.

North End finally got forward and a neat move ended when Bruce headed over the bar from a good cross by Taylor. Preston were grimly clinging on to their advantage, and couldn't seem to sustain any decent period of time in the Rovers half.

Alex Bruce makes room to shoot but his attempt was saved by the Rovers goalkeeper

McKenzie tried a clever back heel around halfway, but was left with egg on his face as Coleman coolly weighed up the situation and came away with the ball to set up a chance for Elliott. Before he could turn towards goal however, Derek Fazackerley nipped in to dispossess the striker. Following a throw-in from the right, Metcalfe's attempt to square the ball across the front of North End's penalty area was intercepted by Potts. Quickly out of the blocks, he went past one man and continued down the middle launching a pass forward for Elliott to chase alongside Rathbone. After the striker made up the ground to get to the ball first, he was brought to earth by the right back on the edge of the penalty area.

Accompanied by more loud cries of, 'come on you yellows,' Bell's floated free kick managed to find Baxter's head but the ball was glanced wide.

As the end of the match loomed on the horizon, a pass from Doyle was taken forward by Bruce down the right. He was confronted by Brian Morley but left the defender for dead and crossed the ball into the box towards Potts, who was beaten to the ball by Parkin.

Loud, rumbustious cheers from the North End fans greeted referee Pat Partridge's final whistle, heralding a rare league 'double' over Rovers.

Football POST
Lancashire Evening Post

How Mick Robinson became a £500,000 STAR
READ NORMAN SHAKESHAFT ON P.4

Our rambles return - by Ullswater
with Womanpost

Strugglers fail in a brave fight-back

SCOREBOARD

ROVERS SHOT DOWN BY ICE-COLD ALEX!

Stiles was a happy man. *"The wind made it very difficult to play good football, but I was pleased with the attitude of our players. I was delighted with the performances of Graham Bell and Steve Elliott, their attitude to the game is right and they are both good players.*

"Alex Bruce's winner was a great goal, worthy to win any match, and he proved once again that he is a First Division player."

That win took North End's impressive unbeaten to streak in the league to 14 matches – their last defeat being way back on November 25th, away at Orient.

In the remaining 11 games of the season, another 11 points were accumulated enabling North End to post a final position of seventh. It was very impressive work by Stiles and Alan Kelly; they were obviously thinkers about the game.

In their first season together, they guided North End back into Division Two. In their second campaign, they not only consolidated North End's position, they steadily and patiently steered the club to its highest league position for 15 years. They were a class act, and needed backing positively.

CHAPTER 28

'LOADSAMONEY' SWALES GETS IN TOUCH

With 15 goals in 48 appearances, Michael Robinson could hardly have the tag of 'Preston North End Legend' placed around his neck. By the end of the 1978/79 season however, nobody watching North End could dispute that he was more than well on the way.

Robinson gave a very revealing interview to the LEP's Norman Shakeshaft towards the end of March 1979 about life at Deepdale after the North End Board had turned down an approach of £300,000 from Queens Park Rangers, and an offer in writing from Manchester City of £350,000.

He became a North End apprentice professional on his 16th birthday, just after leaving school. Other offers from Blackpool and Blackburn Rovers had been binned after receiving an invitation to go to Deepdale from Bobby Charlton. Robinson was impressed with calibre of people at the club at the time, such as Charlton, Nobby Stiles and Alan Kelly – all with international experience to bestow on the ready and willing youngster.

He progressed, and made his first team debut at Cardiff City on April 7th 1976; North End by now managed by Harry Catterick. After another appearance early the following season in the League Cup at Bury it became clear to Robinson that the manager wanted to get rid of him.

After hitting Robinson with a no-holds-barred salvo saying he was *'too soft'* (vernacular words omitted), Catterick then really marked the hopeful's card. Furnishing chairman Alan Jones with his opinion that Robinson *'had a low pain barrier and wasn't aggressive enough,'* he wanted Robinson out of the club on a free transfer.

Robinson did have one person on his side though.

"Catterick said I was finished – and it was only Alan Kelly who spoke up for me and kept me at the club."

Kelly took the youngster under his wing, showed faith in him and gave him confidence.

"Kell came back with me in the afternoons for extra training and also worked me on my days off. He had me sprinting, shooting, heading – he would kick hundreds of balls up in the air for me to challenge Mick Baxter for the ball.

"He would give me crosses and passes and make me shoot with my weaker foot, as well as getting me to knock the ball off in tight situations.

"He bullied me at times but I have to thank him for everything. My form has improved through sheer hard work and the practice he gave me."

With this impressive mentoring, Robinson was in a good place to succeed when his next first team chance came along, after blossoming in the reserves after Catterick had gone.

"I am 13 stones and six foot tall, and I know that if I can keep my speed I will be difficult to stop as I have been blessed with a good stature. Alan told me it would be silly not to use my physique. I had never realised the advantage it gave me, but I make the most of it now. He never lets me relax, and gives me a kick in the pants every time he thinks I am doing.

"He still works with me in the afternoons and on my days off, and has told me I should come off the field after a game with nothing left.

"I'll always remember one special thing Alan told me. He said that to be a centre forward, you have got to put your head where you are prepared to have it kicked, telling me that you can always mend your head, but you might not get the chance to score another goal!

"What he meant is that there must be no half measures in my displays and I have tried to give everything ever since."

Robinson's return to the first team started promisingly at the back end of 1977/78, with encouragement from both Mike Elwiss and Alex Bruce.

"I think they were glad to have a big player alongside them in attack. They carried me through and things worked well. I have continued to play just how Kell taught me in the reserves and this season has been great.

"I was sorry to see Mike Elwiss go, but I did not replace him as he was a very different type of player to me – although I try and work as hard as he did."

Despite those offers for Robinson's services from Queens Park Rangers and Manchester City just a few weeks previously, apparently he was still fully on board with North End and had high hopes.

"Now I'm looking forward to the future and believe North End can win promotion to the First Division next season."

Perhaps it's pure coincidence, but we will never know if that early Division One interest in Robinson hastened North End's signing of Steve Elliott from Nottingham Forest. He made his debut for Preston on March 17th – a week or two after QPR's enquiry.

Manchester City's owner was Peter Swales. He was the archetypal northern achiever type; with a business partner he had grown a small sheet music business into a flourishing television and electrical retail empire, and at the right moment sold out to 'megacorp' Thorn Electronics, for a very tidy sum.

He had a reputation for firing Manchester City managers on a whim, indeed in his first season in control, three bit the dust. Tony Book, a long-time servant of the club as player and coach, took over from the last of those incumbents, Ron Saunders, and somehow then managed to stay in the job for three years. Despite guiding them to runners-up spot in Division One in 1976/77, and fourth the following season, he was sidelined in favour of Malcolm Allison who had recently returned to the club as Book's assistant. Before Allison officially took over in summer of 1979, he had convinced Swales to massively invest.

Why is all this relevant? It's because both Swales and Allison thought big; brashly big. If they wanted something, they had to have it – and boy, did they want Michael Robinson!

Swales telephoned the North End chairman Alan Jones, following up his rejected written bid of £350,000. Jones told him that he hadn't even bothered to call a board meeting about the City offer, (probably as it was so close to the QPR offer which had been rejected beforehand).

"Would you organise a board meeting for £450,000?" was Swales' riposte, to which Jones replied "No."

Amazingly, Swales immediately asked the same question, but upped the offer to £550,000. At this point Jones agreed to call a board meeting during which manager Nobby Stiles expressed his wish not to sell.

Was this a ploy to extract further funds from City? Stiles would have been fully conversant with the football scene in Manchester and will have surely have had knowledge of what to expect from Swales and Allison if North End played hard to get.

If that was the case, it worked. When informed by Jones that the offer had been refused, Swales instantly increased the offer to £650,000 – triggering yet another North End Board meeting.

Amongst all this rapid to-ing and fro-ing, Robinson had been kept fully informed and quite understandably now had the desire to leave North End for the bright lights of Division One.

An astounded North End Board this time accepted City's offer when they met, and then pushed their luck with one last proviso. Swales was told that the offer was only acceptable if City also paid the VAT element of the deal – in the region of an additional £90,000. Unbelievably, this was agreed to straight away and so it was that City – effectively self-rinsing themselves of £756,000 in cash – made 20 year old Robinson, for a time at least, the second most expensive footballer ever in Britain.

Considering Robinson was still developing as a player and had no top flight experience, the fee that City were only too willing to part with was generally seen as extravagant. *'A player is worth what you are willing to pay for him,'* is the oft-heard maxim, but did Swales and Allison really know what they were doing?

Just a few months later, they splashed out £1.47 million on Wolverhampton Wanderers midfielder Steve Daley and again faced lengthy questions as to their sanity.

Within a year Robinson was sold on to Brighton & Hove Albion, at an estimated loss of over £500,000, but this was small beer to the loss on Daley, who lasted 20 months at Maine Road before being transferred to Seattle Sounders at a deficit of £1.17 million.

Though it was to be that Robinson spent just a small part of his career at Preston North End, it was certainly an exciting time from a spectator's point of view. Alas, he joined a long list of youthful talent that the loyal North End fans were allowed nothing more than a glimpse of.

Once again, in June 1979, we were left thinking 'if only...'and, just as importantly, 'thank goodness for Alan Kelly,' because if it hadn't been for his vision, Catterick's poor judgement would have deprived the club of £756,000!

'KELLY RESCUED ME,' SAYS MICK

JOINING THE IN CROWD..

Mick Robinson at Maine Road yesterday.

£750,000 SPLASH

By BOB RUSSELL

MANCHESTER CITY'S Malcolm Allison last night justified his club's record pay-out for £750,000 Preston unknown Mick Robinson.

Allison, the City assistant manager, explained: "We've now got ourselves one of the few, true centre forwards. A real rarity these days. And at twenty we've also got him at just the right time.

"He's just beginning to blossom and he's got both the attributes and the attitude of a potentially great player—not which he already is."

City manager Tony Book said: "No doubt there will be people saying we are paying a terrible lot of money for a comparatively unknown player. But this boy is one of the best.

"Once our fans have seen him in action I'm certain they'll agree we've bought a great player."

Robinson becomes the second most costly player in Britain after only one full season of Second Division football in which he scored 17 goals.

The Leicester-born striker said last night: "I'm an ambitious player and delighted to be joining such a great go-ahead club."

A £756,000 swoop for Robinson

MANCHESTER CITY are paying a staggering £756,000 to Second Division Preston for 20-year-old striker Mick Robinson.

And that makes Robinson, who was in the Central League side just two seasons ago, Britain's second most expensive player behind £1 million Trevor Francis.

City were not the only club interested in Robinson, who scored 14 League goals last season despite a lengthy injury spell.

MICK ROBINSON

QPR had already been rejected by the ambitious youngster and Tottenham were also in the hunt.

But City manager Tony Book, after having a £630,000 bid rejected by Charlton's Mick Flanagan, knew he had to strike fast and pay high.

All set

His first bid for Robinson was £350,000 and Preston said no. Now Book has had to reach for the sky—with the VAT for the deal alone amounting to £90,000 and Robinson collecting £33,000.

Meanwhile unhappy Flanagan looks set for America with New England Teamen agreeing to Charlton's £630,000 asking price.

Teamen coach Noel Cantwell has flown to Britain for talks with the England B striker.

● NEWCASTLE have signed Norwich full-back Ian Davies for £175,000.

The rapid move was made after Davies flew to Tyneside for a medical and talks with Newcastle manager Bill McGarry.

CUP BAN LIFTED

LEEDS have had their three-year F.A. Cup ban lifted after little more than a season.

The FA, who had decided Leeds should play all Cup matches away from home, now accept that their spectators' behaviour has improved.

But the change of heart has come with a warning that they will act firmly if fans get out of hand again.

Credit: Daily Mirror

Credit: Daily Express

CHAPTER 29

1979/80

CHARLTON ATHLETIC V PRESTON NORTH END
AUGUST 18TH 1979

Off to a flier

North End's pre-season form for the 1979/80 season was strong. Five games unbeaten had done much to bolster the confidence of the squad and indeed the fans, expectant after the previous season's performance on the field.

The only new arrivals at Deepdale on time for the big kick-off were John Blackley, a shrewd defender signed on a free transfer from Newcastle United and John Anderson – another defender – arriving just before the start of the season from West Bromwich Albion following an independent tribunal decision to set his transfer fee at £40,000.

Opening day opponents Charlton Athletic, hadn't performed at all well in preparation for the new season, and had already been removed from the League Cup by Peterborough United of Division Four before the league season had begun! Hopes were therefore high that North End would, for once, make a strong start to the campaign.

The contest, at The Valley saw North End field a strong team, albeit without the formidable Alex Bruce who was still a few weeks away from peak fitness following a necessary close-season knee operation, and Don O'Riordan nearing the end of his latest loan spell at Tulsa Roughnecks in the United States. The line-up was therefore:-

Tunks, Taylor, Wilson, Doyle, Baxter, Blackley, Bell, Haselgrave, Elliott, Potts, Thomson. Substitute: Coleman.

Sean Haselgrave was named as skipper, with club captain Francis Burns omitted from the final 12 players, as the game began in a constant drizzle making conditions slippery underfoot on the hard surface.

A crowd of only 6,148 – maybe a reflection of the apathy for Charlton Athletic in south east London – paid to see the game but it was the home side that made the early running. An early corner was won on the left, but striker Martin Robinson's header from the flag kick went well wide of the mark, which in fact set the tone of the game for the rest of the afternoon as far as Charlton were concerned.

The play became confined to midfield, but then North End struck out of the blue, taking the lead on 18 minutes with a goal from Steve Elliott – his first in the league for North End – following a corner from the right.

As the ball arrived into the centre of the Charlton box, Gary Churchouse made an almighty hash of attempting to clear the ball that had been flicked on by Mick Baxter. Elliott moved in swiftly to drive the ball cleanly into the net to spare any further lumbering embarrassment for the midfielder.

There was barely time to take in the fact that the home crowd were already shouting derogatory comments towards their manager, before North End struck again on 23 minutes thus heaping even more pressure on the hapless Andy Nelson.

Ricky Thomson robbed Churchouse in midfield and sent Eric Potts away down the left with a glorious pass. The diminutive striker then launched a shot at the Charlton goal, the surprise of which only enabled goalkeeper Nicky Johns to parry the ball directly into the path of the more than grateful Graham Bell, who hammered the ball into the net from close range.

Two challenges of little finesse by Dave Shipperley on Steve Elliott

More derision and abuse from the home fans had the effect of stirring the home team into action. A determined if rather unfruitful spell of pressure on the North End goal only produced one moment of real concern, when North End had to scramble the ball away following a Roy Tunks fend from a strong drive from Churchouse.

North End soon recovered and Elliott's progress was halted suddenly down the middle by Dick Tydeman, who had his name taken by the referee as due reward for a poor challenge.

Roy Tunks demonstrates the art of goalkeeping – much to the dismay of the home fans

Back the home side came, shots from Phil Warman and Derek Hales were comfortably blocked and cleared by a North End team that seemed content to let the home team huff and puff without incurring any panic whatsoever – then place the home team into fear and dread when they regained possession.

As the half time whistle blew, the home team and manager were subjected to barracking while Preston walked off the pitch two goals up without really trying! North End's football and game management was of a far higher quality than that of Charlton; there was a very evident gulf between the teams.

The second half began with the Charlton substitute on the field for crocked leading scorer Derek Hales, who had twisted his knee in the first half and wasn't showing any signs of recovery.

Quickly out of the traps at the recommencement, Charlton flew at North End quite obviously following an 'earful' from the manager. Just as before these were snuffed out one by one, before a slick North End move enabled Stephen Doyle to split the home defence with a through ball for Potts. Opting to shoot long and catch Johns on the hop, his 25 yard attempt whistled just wide.

Preston's neat passing and movement all around the pitch was inciting the home fans to return to jeering their own team, as they were being made to look distinctly inferior. Elliott was notable up front for North End, making several productive runs and opening up space for his teammates to flood into.

It was Elliott again in the thick of things when he ran forward and chested down a free kick from Harry Wilson to the feet of Thomson; his first time shot going inches over the bar.

Charlton retaliated and Lawrie Madden became another home player to shoot hopelessly wide of the North End goal. A few minutes later, another cross into the North End box following a John Blackley handball was again met by Madden – and was again headed well wide of the post.

The home voices of discontent were now echoing around the empty stadium, and to make matters worse, North End thumped the third goal in after 71 minutes.

A forward pass down the middle from Doyle to Potts was the signal for Elliott to glide across the box and take a couple of defenders with him, thus opening up an ocean of space behind. Thomson was also homing in, and it was he who beat Johns with a well placed shot after Potts had slid the ball into his path.

It was as simple as blinking! The goal was a fully deserved reward for North End who had demonstrated to their hosts how to 'boss' a game of football.

Elliott had in fact given his designated marker, Dave Shipperley a torrid afternoon. The big defender who was forever struggling to keep up with the North End centre forward, put in a performance that could only be described as 'clunky' at best.

Charlton restarted as the home fans were loudly demanding the head of manager Andy Nelson from the sidelines. They managed two tepid approaches towards the North End goal, but Tunks saved easily from Robinson on both occasions.

The game drew to a close with the echoes of 'Nelson Out! Nelson Out!' bouncing off the walls of the vast, sparsely populated stadium that had once accommodated 71,000 for a game of football. It was very much a case of 'job done' by North End, and for once a Lilywhites campaign was off to a flying start.

By the time of the return fixture with Charlton Athletic at Deepdale on November 3rd, Nelson had been relieved of his duties and a few of the squad culled.

Calmness personified, Stiles said after match, *"I thought all the lads played well and was very pleased with the performance. We have an injury worry concerning Steve Elliott that we could have done without though. He injured his ankle before half time and soldiered on but we will have a closer look when we get back."*

By the time Burnley visited Deepdale for the derby clash on October

WEEKEND Leisure and Football POST

Lancashire Evening Post

No. 28,742 SATURDAY AUGUST 18, 1979 9p

INSIDE

CAN P.N.E. WIN ANYTHING THIS SEASON?

Plus

SCORED

What a start to season!

PNE SHINE IN THREE GOAL BLAST OFF

PRESTON North End began their new League campaign in Division Two in fine style by beating Charlton Athletic 3-0 at The Valley today.

By Norman Shakeshaft

20th, North End were sat in 10th position, within a couple of wins of the leading pack. It had been a decent start to the season; Preston had only lost two of their 11 games so far and were still very hard to defeat, but the fact they had only won three of the remaining nine matches was slightly worrying.

The basis for success was clearly there. If they had converted just three of their six draws to date into wins by scoring three more goals in those contests, Preston would have been sat in joint second position in Division Two.

The management team of Nobby Stiles and Alan Kelly had done their part. Nobody rode roughshod over North End on the field anymore, but with Michael Robinson gone, Alex Bruce not quite finding his mojo after a summer knee operation and Steve Elliott's goals drying up somewhat, it was obvious what was missing.

The club wasn't broke either. The AGM revealed the club was in the black to the tune of £450,000. After years of hearing that the club, '*...has been forced to sell because of pressure from the bank*' there now was no pressure from the bank – and nobody arriving who would strengthen the team either – save Paul McGhee, a lively player, but nevertheless a budget buy brought in during late October to bolster the attack. He returned eight goals by the end of the season.

Surely Stiles and Kelly actually deserved backing a little more firmly than that considering their achievements, but nothing from the boardroom was forthcoming.

It's incredible to think that with today's equivalent of £2.2 million lying in the bank and transfer fees not as inflated as today's, that more effort wasn't made to help them. Investing in just one decent striker could have made all the difference, and taken North End even further forward.

There was however, another financial nightmare looming on the horizon for North End that would see all their bank funds and plenty more besides eaten up. It was the beginning of the period that would bring the club to its knees by the mid Eighties.

Promotion from Division Three in 1977/78 meant that several more sections of the *Safety of Sports Grounds Act 1975* became applicable to North End. This was an Act that had taken several years to evolve, (and was continually amended after it was initially passed in Parliament), mainly as an outcome of the Ibrox Park crowd disaster of 1971.

Records show that North End spent around just £10,000 on ground safety and improvements between 1977 and 1979, but this then ramped up considerably – reaching £317,000 in 1979/80 and a further £171,000 in the following year. On top of that a grant of £210,000 was swallowed up, as the letter of the law was applied.

'Ah,' I hear you say, 'that's why there was no money available to strengthen the team.' Well, yes, and no.

I think everybody who went to watch football on the grand old version of Deepdale in the Seventies would agree that decades of neglect and non-investment by the board had seen to it that it was well past its sell-by date. Was it not throwing precious good money after bad by paying for *all* this necessary safety work, when perhaps sections of the ground could have been permanently closed?

Even when the wonderful new barriers had been installed at a huge premium, the very same section of the ground was again closed in subsequent seasons as it had failed elsewhere!

A major decision concerning the Deepdale stadium was needed – but none was made. That problem was passed on to the next generation of directors.

By buying Deepdale back they could surely have used it as collateral and perhaps even started a step by step demolish and replace programme, rather than lose the best part of an equivalent of £3.5 million in just a few years on what amounted to nothing more than applying sticking plaster repairs to a relentless, escalating, unstoppable decay.

Deepdale 1979

The club crest panel that sat at the centre on front of the Pavilion Stand after it had replaced the clock in the early Sixties

Deepdale 1979

Two areas of Deepdale that would eventually be cordoned off despite continual and expensive remedial work. Top: The rear portion of the Kop. Bottom: The area of the Kop that ran around to meet the Pavilion Paddock.

Credit for photographs on pages 246 & 247: Will Gibson

CHAPTER 30

1979/80

PRESTON NORTH END V BURNLEY
OCTOBER 20TH 1979

Thomson secures the points

It was a busy news weekend for the town of Preston and indeed Great Britain. On consecutive days, major headlines were catching the eye at the newspaper stands, and not just about football!

First, Preston Council had voted to finally close the financially hit Preston Docks. This was followed the next day by a call to the *LEP* offices from a man claiming he was the 'Yorkshire Ripper.' He wasn't, but thankfully this time-waster was finally caught and imprisoned many years later. Finally, in Australia, the Brisbane police were detaining a man they thought could be Lord Lucan – who had disappeared from Britain after being suspected of murder.

A good old Lancashire 'derby' was just what was needed after that lot, and the clash with our East Lancashire neighbours saw 12,300 fans click through the turnstiles to witness a North End win which took the team up to eighth position in Division Two.

On the eve of the match, Burnley reported that rampaging winger Steve Kindon was fit enough to return to action following a lay-off. They needed him, as the Clarets were desperate men. Sat at the bottom of the table, they had hadn't won in the past 24 outings – over half a season! During the week they had sacked manager Harry Potts, replacing him with Brian Miller and assistant Frank Caspar.

Surely this was a home banker...?

"The fact that a change has taken place will make things a lot more difficult for us," said Stiles, adding, *"the longer they have gone without a win makes you feel that they must win a match very soon."*

Stiles and Kelly named the following line-up:-

Tunks, Taylor, Cameron, Burns, Baxter, Blackley, Bell, Haselgrave, Elliott, Thomson, Bruce. Substitute: Potts

North End Kicked off towards the Kop and set off full of intent – in fact taking only three minutes to puncture the Burnley defensive balloon and take the lead. The visitors' defence looked decidedly anxious as North End's latest emerging star, Ricky Thomson, moved forward to take control of the ball on the edge of the Burnley box.

In the course of gliding past two tackles, Thomson was driven towards the by-line on the right side. His attempted cross into the goalmouth rebounded off defender Derek Scott and looped to Sean Haselgrave on the opposite side of the goal, whereupon he calmly centred the ball to near post finding Alex Bruce who had the simple task of nodding the ball into the net to put North End one up.

Haselgrave was in focus once again a few minutes later, this time in midfield where he body-checked Leighton James just as he looked to be getting into full stride. Martin Dobson swung the free kick into the North End box, but it was too high for the leaping Brian Noble, and passed through for a goal kick.

North End were looking dangerous, and twice within a few minutes Steve Elliott was put through by the dominant North End midfield. The first half chance was eventually cleared by Ian Brennan but when Graham Bell launched a pass for the centre forward to run on to, it saw him skillfully move to the right and launch a low centre that fizzed across the Burnley goalmouth – sadly without a North End toe in sight to prod the ball in to the open goal.

Top: Ricky Thomson carves his way through the Burnley defence which led to...

Left: ...Alex Bruce opening the scoring for North End with a header

Indeed, Elliott was buzzing and shortly afterwards hit another fierce drive that produced a spectacular save by Alan Stevenson. It seemed only a matter of time before North End would double their lead, but then out of the blue, Burnley equalised.

Martin Dobson, a strolling, classy midfielder brought the visitors back to parity when his 25 yard shot was deflected off Mick Baxter and into the North End net past the rooted Roy Tunks. It was one of those incidents that seem so unjust in the game of football, let's just say that neither side deserved to be level at this juncture!

Nevertheless, Burnley seemed more competitive for a short time after the goal, but North End were still looking the most likely to score as pressure once again mounted on the Burnley defence.

Billy Rodaway cleared the ball off the Burnley line following a shot from Baxter and then Danny Cameron intercepted the dodgiest of clearances by Stevenson, turning over the ball to Bruce. After a couple of strides a low 25 yard shot was despatched at the Burnley goal, but somehow Stevenson recovered enough composure to get a boot to the ball and deflect it for a corner.

Ricky Thomson puts North End back into the lead

With half time just seconds away, Bell – a real energy in the North End midfield – put Thomson through. When the shot came it wasn't hit sweetly with his left foot but it somehow deceived Stevenson, and his bungled attempt at a save couldn't prevent the ball from rolling under him and entering the net.

Much joy all round in the West Paddock – the perfect time to score! The half time whistle blew before Burnley could restart the game.

During half time I made my way down towards the Town End hopefully following the North End action, although it did cross my mind fleetingly that this was North End – and there were never any guarantees!

The first incident of any note in the second half was when Stevenson slipped while retrieving a wayward back pass, but it was too wide for North End to take advantage of.

Burnley – wouldn't you just know it – settled into a much brighter pattern of play and most of the action was now at the Kop end of the ground. John Blackley was soon forced to concede a corner after the powerful Steve Kindon had charged forward down the left flank and crossed the ball into the North End penalty area.

The ball was eventually cleared and North End tried to pick up from where they had left off in the first half. Elliott managed to drive in a shot that was on the way into the net but was blocked by the outstretched leg of Rodaway, just feet from the line.

Back came Burnley, with Noble sliding a ball forward to put Kindon away. The big winger outpaced the North End back line to burst clear but when confronted by Tunks racing out of goal, he delivered a shanked shot that was more of a problem for the press photographers than the North End goalkeeper.

Preston had certainly gone off the boil, and it was Paul Fletcher who troubled them next when he beat three defenders down the right before delivering a centre that thankfully was cleared with the minimum of fuss by Baxter.

Derek Scott, the Burnley right back, was now getting forward more often and with good approach work set up Fletcher and then James, but both forwards squandered their chances.

At this point, Stiles had seen enough and replaced Elliott with the livewire Eric Potts, hoping to inject some verve back into the North End attack. Little impression was made by the home team after the substitution however, and the plan seemed to have failed altogether when with just 10 minutes left, Burnley drew level.

A free kick on the perimeter of the North End box was curled in by James and led to an almighty goalmouth scramble before Fletcher managed to turn the ball back to James who slammed in the equaliser with a low drive.

A minute later, just when our sinking hearts had descended to their lowest level, North End were stung into action and somehow manufactured a goal to put their noses back in front.

It all began when Potts made enough room to deliver a low 15 yard shot that was blocked on the goal line by Brennan, the ball then pinging around the Burnley goalmouth accompanied by the screams of the home crowd. Eventually it fell to Thomson on the left, who drilled in a low shot that hit the back of the net after beating Stevenson's dive.

This set up a grandstand finish to the game, with chances spurned at both ends. Potts had the crowd on their feet when he whizzed in and out of a couple of Burnley defenders before skimming a low cross across the face of goal that just beat the outstretched boot of Bruce.

At the other end, after another mazy run, a Kindon cross was met by an header from Noble that grazed the outside of the North End post.

There was much relief all around Deepdale when the referee brought matters to completion. Who would have thought that the match could have ended so close after the way it had started, with North End so dominant and Burnley's defence shakier than a jelly on top of a washing machine?

Leisure and Football POST
Lancashire Evening Post
No. 28,796 SATURDAY OCTOBER 20, 1979 9p

INSIDE
JIMMY ARMFIELD LOOKS AT ENGLAND'S WORLD CUP OPPONENTS - Page 4

PLUS

Prizes with Junior Post

Bruce, Thomson on target

PNE CLINCH IT IN LATE GOAL BURST

Preston North End 3, Burnley 2

PRESTON plunged Lancashire neighbours Burnley into even deeper relegation trouble with a 3-2 win at Deepdale today. It wasn't an impressive performance by North End who seemed to go completely off the boil in the second half and allow their bottom-of-the-table opponents back into the game.

By Steve Skidmore

SCOREBOARD

Afterwards, Stiles paid tribute to Thomson for this performance and brace of goals, and also had a few words of encouragement for the Burnley manager. *"We were in a similar position last year, but if they keep playing like they did against us they can get out of trouble."*

Alas, they didn't and were relegated along with Charlton Athletic at the end of the season.

CHAPTER 31

NOBBY STILES – A SPECIAL MANAGER

Nobby Stiles, Alan Kelly and the playing squad waved goodbye to the Seventies by delivering in the last two seasons of that era the best on-field performance in terms of North End's league position since the mid-Sixties.

Back then there was managerial stability at the club with Jimmy Milne occupying the first six years of that decade, but all that changed when his successor, Bobby Seith was sacked in April 1970.

Stiles could point to the fact that he had been the longest serving of the four who had given it a go since Seith; three full seasons in the manager's revolving chair at Deepdale was no mean achievement. He had been a godsend for North End.

Brought in as a player who was ready to move into coaching by long time friend and Manchester United and England teammate Bobby Charlton, he brought determination on the pitch in the early years, then drew upon and applied his trove of top level football experience when he was appointed as manager.

Promotion came for North End in Stiles' first season in charge, albeit by the skin of their teeth. This was followed by two excellent seasons in

Division Two, with satisfying finishes of seventh in 1978/79, and 10th in 1979/80, deserving of a more positive backing than was going to be provided in 1980/81 by the board of directors.

The tone of the North End AGM, held in late 1980 didn't exactly convey the feeling that there was help or indeed hope for Stiles on the way. The theme of the meeting was *'no wastage,'* with the board announcing that the club's youth hostel would be closed down in the spring of 1981.

They didn't stop there.

They had already decided what they thought Stiles and Kelly could manage with, and announced that the playing staff would now be restricted to, *"two goalkeepers, four full backs, four central defenders, six midfielders, five forwards, five first year professionals and five apprentices."* As these areas were all covered there would be no immediate need for incoming players.

These annual meetings give a snapshot of how things are at a club, and the only conclusion to draw from this is that the situation for the beginning of the Eighties was desperate. Instead of tackling the big issue of the declining Deepdale, the policy of 'patch up and repair' to satisfy *The Safety of Sports Grounds Act 1975* continued. Pursuing this course of action eventually flipped a healthy £300,000 surplus in 1979 into a deficit of £340,000 by 1981.

It's little wonder that with such doom and gloom emanating from the boardroom not even Stiles and Kelly could beat the policy of little investment, and after a disastrous season, North End returned to Division Three on May 6th 1981.

The North End Board's next move was quite extraordinary. They decided to play what was tantamount to 'football poker' with the remaining scant resources they had left at their disposal. Get this move wrong, and the abyss would be clearly in view!

Within a day or two of North End's relegation, the board who had surely decided Stiles' fate, kept him hanging by a thread until June 5th – by which time they had concluded negotiations with Sydney Olympic to secure the services of...Tommy Docherty! I am still unclear in my mind why popular – but unknowledgeable – 'taproom' opinion was followed by a board usually so dour and restrained.

Roy Tunks knew what Docherty's management style was like. The long serving North End goalkeeper told the LEP in later years, *"I was disappointed when Tommy came in because there were 10 or 11 of us that were separated, and were in the away dressing room – we called it 'the leper colony.'*

"I don't know why he wanted rid of us, but he obviously didn't last long as manager.

"I always remember he came in at Rotherham and did the same. He told the chairman he would get them out of the division, and he did. They got relegated."

After denying Stiles the chance to redeem himself – and paying him compensation of £30,000 for the privilege, the board had also spent £37,000 to buy Docherty out of his Sydney Olympic contract. Alan Kelly, the North End bastion who had the club's interests, hopes and dreams coursing through his veins, unselfishly saved the club £28,000 by deciding to stay on at Deepdale in a coaching capacity.

Just 165 days later, Docherty was fired. It must have been one of those classic, *'if only we could go back in time,'* moments for the board.

Stiles joins the jobless

NOBBY STILES was sacked by Preston yesterday.

Stiles is the fourth member of England's World Cup winning side of 1966 to get the boot from management this year, joining Alan Ball (Blackpool), Geoff Hurst (Chelsea) and Martin Peters (Sheffield United).

Former Everton boss Gordon Lee is favourite for the post.

IAN PORTERFIELD filled one of those vacant managers' seats yesterday when he took over at Fourth Division Sheffield United.

RON ATKINSON looks as if he will be forced to quit as West Brom manager before he can become Manchester United's No. 1. Talks over compensation between the two clubs' chairmen ended in deadlock yesterday.

MALCOLM ALLISON, sacked by Manchester City and Crystal Palace last season, is considering joining Sporting Lisbon as coach.

Now they had to pay off both Docherty and his assistant Ken Shiletto, and appoint yet another manager, Gordon Lee all within six months of sacking Stiles. The doomsday scenario for North End – both on and off the pitch – would continue to loom ever larger until the slide was temporarily halted with the arrival of John McGrath in 1986.

Stiles' immediate response to his dismissal was rather reflective. *"Of course it hurts, but I have no ill feeling towards the club. I wish the new man all the best, and still think this can be a very good club."*

That was so typical of him.

Unknown to many at the time as North End struggled to maintain a foothold in Division Two in 1981, Stiles had suffered health issues no doubt exacerbated by the stress of his task, and lack of boardroom help.

He revealed in a later interview with the LEP that after one particular heavy board meeting towards the end of his Deepdale reign, he came away feeling drained and exhausted.

"My blood pressure was going through the roof and the doctor told me I was heading for a massive heart attack.

"I was 39, and wondering what was going on. It was just a mighty struggle, and I was slipping into trouble, dangerously so.

"It was a Friday, and we had a game the following day. The doctor insisted that I should take the day off, so I went to bed – and slept for 27 hours.

"I did take a step back following that, and maybe it affected my passion. When the sack came, after relegation a few months later, I realised it was probably not the worst thing that could have happened."

"I had eight years playing and managing at Preston but that last 12 months was awful. We needed to win at Derby in our last game to stay up. Alex Bruce scored twice to give us a 2-1 victory, but the champions, West Ham, could only draw at our nearest relegation rivals Cardiff, and that point kept Cardiff up. I knew we'd beat Derby, but deep down I also

knew the Cardiff result wouldn't go our way.

"We had some smashing lads in that dressing room. Brucey, the late Mick Baxter, Steve Elliott, Sean Haselgrave and Roy Tunks, and I cried along with them and our supporters that night.

"Then North End gave me the sack, but that's football."

The interviewer found Stiles, *'...a warm hearted, genuine man,'* a sentiment echoed by those who played for him.

Sean Haselgrave – *"Nobby Stiles was a super manager to play for and a lovely man. I thought the world of Nobby and the rest of the lads did too, there was no edge or ego to the man. He was a very humane individual, who was passionate about his football and loved his players."*

Mike Elwiss – *"Nobby Stiles was the nicest guy I ever met in the game and the best manager. He was very honest and humble and there was no edge to him. He meant a great deal to me and still does."*

As a North End fan who witnessed those times, it pleases me to read and relay such testimonials. He obviously made such a special and lasting impression on those he worked with, and was undoubtedly North End's manager of the decade.

Nobby Stiles speaking to the media at Deepdale in 1978

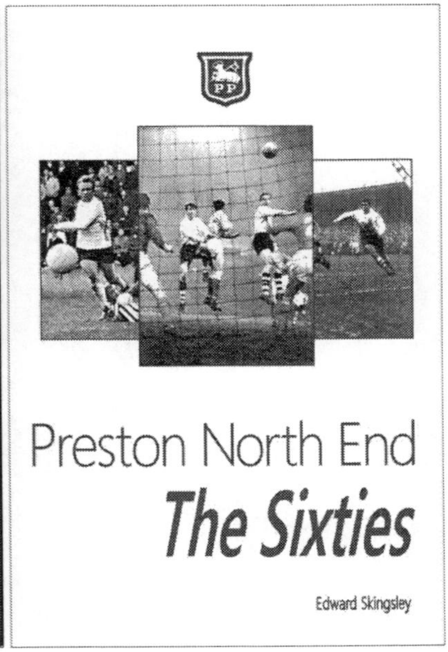

BY THE SAME AUTHOR

ABOUT THE AUTHOR

A North End fan!

REAR COVER PICTURE KEY

Left to right, row 1

Alan Ball and players at PNE photocall July 1970, Ricky Heppolette heads North End's winner at Fulham May 1st 1971, Alan Spavin 1971, Football Post December 11th 1971, Graham Hawkins and Hugh McIlmoyle celebrate the centre forwards second goal against Fulham August 21st 1971.

Left to right, row 2

Bobby Charlton and players at PNE photocall July 1973, Francis Burns goes close against Sunderland October 13th 1973, Evening Post front page February 5th 1972, George Lyall and John McMahon challenge Manchester United's Denis Law February 5th 1972

Left to right, row 3

Bobby Charlton announces playing comeback, Bobby Charlton in action for North End against Crystal Palace September 24th 1974, Bobby Charlton announces resignation August 21st 1975, Mick Baxter 1974

Left to right, row 4

Sean Haselgrave, Alex Bruce scoring against Derby County January 16th 1979, Mike Elwiss 1976, Roy Tunks clasps hold of the ball against Charlton Athletic August 18th 1979

Left to right, row 5

Nobby Stiles in midfield for North End 1973/74, Michael Robinson 1978, Alan Kelly pictured in 1973 (Credit: EFL), Alex Bruce and his shadow, Mick Rathbone March 24th 1979

Bottom picture – *Cover of Evening Post souvenir edition, April 1978*

31793073R00157

Printed in Poland
by Amazon Fulfillment
Poland Sp. z o.o., Wrocław